THE ORIGIN, CAREER AND DESTRUCTION OF THE KELLY GANG

NED KELLY THE BUSHRANGER

F. HUNTER

ETT IMPRINT

Exile Bay

This edition published by ETT Imprint, Exile Bay 2018

First published by A.T. Hodgson, Adelaide 1895.Fourth Edition 1900.

ETT IMPRINT
PO Box R1906
Royal Exchange NSW 1225
Australia

Copyright © this edition ETT Imprint 2018

ISBN 978-1-925706-61-1 (ebook)
ISBN 978-1-925706-60-4 (paper)

Cover: Ned Kelly, the day after he beat Wild Wright. August 8 1874. Photograph by J.J. Chidley, Melbourne Portrait Rooms.

Design by Hanna Gotlieb

CONTENTS

PUBLISHER'S PREFACE

An impartial work, and one which can be depended on as to its data, upon such an interesting episode of Colonial History as that of the Career of the Kelly Gang, has long been enquired for. Great research has resulted in producing a book which, without making heroes of desperadoes, gives all the interesting details and historical facts relating to the origin and destruction of the Kellys and their fellow outlaws.

The Publisher begs the Proprietors of the *Argus* and *Australasian* for their kind permission to copy and use the engravings which appeared in the *Sketcher* re the Kelly Gang.

A.T. HODGSON.
54 FLINDERS STREET,
ADELAIDE, DECEMBER, 1895.

THE ORIGIN, CAREER
AND DESTRUCTION
OF THE KELLY GANG.

At this law-abiding period, it seems difficult to realise how short a time has elapsed since the four men who formed the Kelly Gang kept the whole colony in turmoil and terror. Instinctive criminality in their cases seems to have been fostered and developed in every way by surroundings and circumstances. Having once put themselves into the power of the police, they seem also to have put themselves under the influence of a spirit of dogged hatred and revenge, which revealed itself in a determined defiance of all the restrictions the law would impose. This secured them the homage of that class of society to which the law-breaker is the hero of modern times; and vanity grew by what it fed on, until the whole colony rang with their fiendish exploits. Men of the resource and intelligence displayed by the bushrangers in eluding capture for so long, could not be ignorant of the inevitable consequences of their crimes. But uncontrolled by nature, and fired with the passion of notoriety, these had no terrors for them. So the spectacle of the whole law-enforcing machinery of a country being set at naught by four men only was afforded to a wondering world.

Ned and Dan Kelly were the sons of John Kelly, a Tasmanian convict, whose own record proved him no stranger to crime. Marriage with Ellen, third daughter of James Quin, said to be the founder of the Kelly family, was not much of an improvement from a moral point of view, for the Quins were not undistinguished in law breaking. Though to the marriage with John Kelly the general contamination of the Quin family is attributed, it is not easy to see how such could be the case. James Quin was an Irishman, who settled in Victoria with his family in the year 1839, ostensibly as a farmer, managing, however, to so distinguish himself as a cattle-stealer as to become an object of undesired attention to the police. Farming so combined, was sure to pay at that time, whatever it might do in the long run, and in 1863 he sold the property acquired in Wallan Wallan for £2,000, with which he retired to Glenmore Station. This was in that remote part of the North-Eastern district which has since become known to fame as the Kelly Country, and was peculiarly adapted for such a lawless work as from thenceforth was carried on there. James Quin's evil propensities developed early in two of his sons, of whom he had four. These, with six daughters, made up the number of his family, and James and John, the two sons of most unenviable repute at Wallan Wallan, were evidently well fitted to be invaluable as aids in such doubtful operations as were carried on from Glenmore. So it will be seen that the charge of contaminating the Quin family cannot well be brought against John Kelly, though his evil proclivities helped doubtless to strengthen and intensify theirs. Wrong-doing in their case seemed hereditary, and what was in the bone would have to come out in the flesh, though not perhaps to the same extent if no such person as John Kelly had ever allied himself with them.

Kelly was sent out to Tasmania in 1841 for some agrarian outrage committed with murderous intent. He was working as a carpenter at Wallan Wallan when he became connected with the Quins, and similarity of nature and pursuits cemented the bond between them. Kelly abandoned carpentering for gold digging, and was successful enough to gain the means for the purchase of a small property at Beveridge, which soon became the haunt of all the scoundrelism of the district. In 1865 he served a sentence for cattle duffing in the Kilmore Gaol, and did not long survive his release.

Unfortunately for the community at large, Ellen Kelly, *nee* Quin, was in every way fitted to be John Kelly's mate, and, after his death, her place became the resort of all who were most lawlessly inclined. She took up her abode at Eleven-Mile Creek, near Greta, and from there most of the mischief that was brewing for so long before the Kelly outbreak seemed to emanate. The family numbered seven—three sons and four daughters. Two of the sons—Ned and Dan—were destined to a fame that will live as long as there is a criminal in existence to hand it down as glorious to lowest-class posterity; and the third, James, seems to have been as proficient in criminality as the rest of the family. The sisters seem also to have been bold and daring in the extreme. They were evidently devoted to the interests of their brothers and associates, and also inspired with the hatred for the police, and the glory in outwitting them, which characterised most of the desperadoes who gathered at their place. Two of the daughters were married—Mrs. Skillian and Mrs. Gunn. Kate Kelly, who figures prominently in the outlaws' career, and Grace were the other two.

Ned Kelly seems to have been the master spirit of the gang, whit behind his brother in recklessness and determination, though decidedly more bloodthirsty. He is described as low, cunning, and a sneak, and, judging from portraits of him, must have been all that and more. Ned Kelly seems to have gravitated naturally towards men of Power the bushranger's stamp, and to have, from a child, be fired with the desire for like dubious distinction. Power and Glenmore were intimately connected, and Ned Kelly seems to have taken the bushranger for his model. The good opinion was not mutual, however, for Power seemed to think there was more than a strain of cowardice in his youthful aid's nature. After events proved him wofully wrong in this, but to the last there was something akin to contempt in the estimation Ned Kelly was held in by the bushranger. The two were in trouble together more than once, but Ned Kelly always managed to get off, and gradually hardened into the desperado whose name became a terror to all of law-abiding nature. The other members of the gang were Steve Hart, a horse-stealer by profession apparently, and an ill-looking ruffian at best, and Joe Byrne, who seems to have been superior in birth and education to the rest, but to have taken to the life from sheer love of evil. Though endowed with physical and mental power that would have enabled him to succeed in some much more reputable line of life, he preferred the short life and the merry one to which the gang devoted themselves from the first. Long before the outbreak which branded these men with infamy of the worst description, they were a constant source of trouble to those who had the administering of the law. The Quins, the Lloyds, and the Kellys—with the numerous off-shoots of their families, and the kindred spirits around them— soon made the district in which they had elected to settle a dread to all of more law-abiding disposition compelled to settle or to travel near them. So great did the trouble ultimately become that, after the arrest of Power in 1870, the Government yielded to the oft-demonstrated need of a police station in the locality. As Glenmore, which was situated of the track between Mansfield and the Murray, was apparently the hotbed of all the evil, it was decided to erect one near there; and much to the dissatisfaction of the elder Quin and his associates, the station was established forthwith. Two constables were placed in possession, and found their hands full indeed. Great activity prevailed amongst the lawless crowd. Every device that could annoy or inflict loss upon those in charge, or the Government, was resorted to, but without avail. The constables stuck to their posts, and so discharged their duty as to make Quin see the futility of such endeavours to dislodge them. He then sold Glenmore, and took himself out of the district. Given the strength of others, much of the after trouble is distinctly traceable. The district was given over to lawlessness, and there was need for all the safeguards the Government could provide against it. Instead of which, however, it went in for "a penny wise and pound foolish" system, which necessitated the after expenditure of thousands of pounds, as well as in some degree contributed to the terrible tragedies which shocked the community three years later. Oblivious to the really serious state of affairs, however, the Government did away with Glenmore Station, and reduced the strength of others, after which criminality in the district became more rampant every day. Cattle-stealing was what the king of desperadoes (Quin) was most addicted to, and it was carried on almost with impunity, the law seeming powerless to prevent it. Years of immunity brought a sense of security, which made the most timid bold, as well as justified the belief in their own invulnerability and resource, which made the ruffianly bands so difficult to cope with. There seems to have been no rest for the apprehensiveness of the community, and no terrors in the law for evildoers. Matters continued in this unsatisfactory state until April, 1878, when an attempt was made to arrest Dan Kelly; Constable Fitzpatrick, who attempted to execute the warrant, was beguiled into entering Mrs.Kelly's house at Greta, whither he had gone to seek Dan and the cousin Lloyd, who was also implicated. There he met with a determined resistance from the people assembled, and was finally shot in the wrist by Ned Kelly, and compelled to flee. This was premonitory of what was to come. Ned and Dan Kelly betook themselves to the bush; but the other assailants, as well as Mrs. Kelly and Williamson, a near relation, were arrested for the assault upon the constable, and sentenced to long terms imprisonment. Their mother's imprisonment is said to have been the predisposing cause to much that happened afterwards; that it rankled in the minds of her sons, and the morbidly sympathetic of the community found some little excuse fore their after-doings in the thought of filial affection. There is nothing, however, in the Kelly's career to denote that any of the more worthy feelings of human nature ever influenced them. They seem to have been rogues from childhood, and criminals to the core. Hatred of the police, who were the outward and visible signs of the restraints they abhorred, grew with their growth, until it became the master passion of their lives. The severity of the punishment meted out to Mrs. Kelly added fuel to the flames; and Fitzpatrick, who seems to have been regarded with disfavor by friends as well as foes, doubtless exercised his authority with less tact and judgment that was required when dealing with such characters. But what seems far more probable is that the knowledge of their being able to defy the authority they detested, only so long as they were able to keep out of its clutches, spurred them on in their infamous work. To men of such violet and vindictive passions, the need to so often slink away and hide from the power every impulse of their natures urged them to openly defy, must have been almost intolerable. And it is, too, more likely to have been the most predisposing cause of their after-excesses than the alleged persecution of the Kelly family so often put forward as partial justification of the acts which shocked the whole community. Ned Kelly seems to have lost no opportunity of posing as a hero. He was undoubtedly inordinately vain, and also sufficiently well acquainted with the low-class human nature with which he had to deal, to know what would rouse their sympathies most effectually.

MURDER OF SERGEANT KENNEDY AND CONSTABLES LONERGAN AND SCANLON

From April to October little that was authentic was heard of Ned or Dan Kelly. A reward of £100 was offered for their arrest, but it seemed likely to go unclaimed. The Kellys had relations and sympathisers all around them. Hart and Byrne were with them, so it is not to be wondered at that October was well advanced before there was anything positive to go upon. On the 25th of that month one of the parties organised to search the districts in which it was averred the Kellys had been seen, made for the Wombat Ranges, with order to scour them completely. This party was under the command of the ill-fated Sergeant Kennedy, who seems to have been respected by all who came in contact with him, and was completed by Constables Lonergan, Scanlon, and McIntyre. It was more than hinted that there was double treachery on the part of an informant of the Kellys' whereabouts, and that to protect himself from their rage he communicated the fact of their enemies' proximity to them. This has not been borne out, however. The organised search of the suspected districts was suggested to Superintendent Sadlier, who had been placed in charge by Secretary Secretan, and Sergeant Kennedy's suggestions and plans for carrying it out met with the entire approval of his superior officer. Kennedy proposed to establish a depot in the vicinity of the Stringy Bark Creek, from which the parties to be despatched simultaneously from Mansfield and Greta could co-operate. This was done; the Greta party, under Senior-Constable Shoebridge, were sent to search the flat country towards the King River, Fifteen-Mile, and Holland's Creeks; and the party from Mansfield turned their attention to the ranges and creeks.

The site of the proposed depot was selected by Sergeant Kennedy, who was evidently under no apprehension of danger. The possibility of the Kellys being near seems to have never occurred to him, and the whole party were evidently settled in the belief that a tedious search lay between them and any trace of the Kellys. This will in some measure account for the disadvantage at which the party was taken. For the lack of precaution three paid with their lives, and the fourth escaped only by a promptitude of action and readiness of resource that is not often possible to say one at the extreme moment of life. McIntyre has frequently been blamed for what he did, but as his critics usually argued from the safe side of civilization they opinions hardly carry the weight desired. He and Lonergan had been left in camp, and a little after midday were bailed up by four men, two more, be it noted, that they had expected to have to reckon with. McIntyre, who was unarmed, had no resource but to throw up his hands as ordered; but Lonergan seems to have been determined to resist. He was shot dead, and Kennedy and Scanlon, who on their return to camp refused to surrender, shared the same fate. The murder of Kennedy was the most inhuman of all the deeds perpetrated by the gang. Although three brave men fell victims to the Kelly hate and lust for plunder on this occasion, Kennedy was by so far the bravest and the best that the fate of the others is sometimes almost passed over in the tragedy of this. Kennedy had—with what the Commission afterwards characterised as "a singular disregard to possible contingencies"—divided his party; himself and Scanlon going off to prosecute the search for the Kellys together and leaving McIntyre and Lonergan in charge of the camp. But it is to be remembered, that not one of the party had the faintest idea or hope of the Kellys being near them, and none could dream of the lengths to which the gang were prepared to go. There was nothing in their previous career to rouse anticipation of any such cold-blooded atrocity as they afterwards proved themselves capable of. The shooting at Fitzpatrick was regarded as having been done in the flush and heat of passion, and none seemed to think that there was any prospect of such a risky act being deliberately repeated, so all unprepared were the ill-fated three for the fate that overtook them. When Kennedy and Scanlon were gone the other two set about camp work. McIntyre, who had the cooking for the day in hand, had disembarrassed himself of his weapons, so when suddenly confronted by the Kelly Gang, and ordered to throw up his hands, he had no resource but obey. Lonergan, who was armed, instead of doing so, started running with apparently the idea of getting some vantage ground from which to shot. He had only covered four or five yards when he was shot down, and expired a few minutes afterwards. That he meant to show fight was evident by the attempt to get out his revolver when running. According to the evidence given at the trial, the gang manifested some regret at having to shoot down so plucky a fellow. This, however, did not apparently alter their intentions in regard to the rest of the party. Ned Kelly then searched the tent for firearms and anything there might be in it worth taking. When he came back, Dan Kelly, with the ghastly pleasantry which sometimes distinguished him, made a move to handcuff McIntyre, but on the latter appealing against this, as he was already powerless for harm, the handcuffs were not put on. McIntyre than had to wait while the gang had tea, loaded guns, and prepared for the reception of his comrades. During this interval of suspense he had to answer many questions. Ned Kelly asked who the two men were, and McIntyre said,

"Kennedy and Scanlon". He then sought to discover the intentions of the gang. Would they shoot the two constables in cold blood? Ned Kelly said it depended on their surrendering; he would shoot no man who held up his hands and surrendered. This could not have relieved the enquirer much, as he must have known both Kennedy and Scanlon well enough to know that there was more probability of their contesting every inch of ground than of surrendering. McIntyre was ordered to post himself in a conspicuous place, and advised to induce his comrades to surrender. So when the two, unsuspecting of anything that had happened, rode into camp, Kennedy slightly ahead, McIntyre went forward, told them what had happened, and said, "Sergeant, I think you had better dismount and surrender." Instead of doing this, however, they apparently determined instantly to conquer or to die. From the account given of the scene that followed, in Superintendent Hare's book, "The Last of the Bushrangers," it must have been one of such cold-blooded cruelty and pathos that readers are taken back to the ages when "the quality of mercy" was almost unknown. Scanlon was shot while dismounting, and Kennedy, thus left single-handed, seemed to have resolved to sell his life as dearly as possible. He jumped from his horse and began to fire. Ned Kelly said afterwards that Kennedy was the bravest man he had ever met. When Scanlon fell, McIntyre, expecting no mercy from any one, caught Kennedy's horse as it bolted past, and with a presence of mind which afterwards subjected him to many insinuations of cowardice, made good his escape. The hapless sergeant was thus left to the mercy of his enemies. Ned Kelly said he fought as long as he had a shot left to fight with, but this fact did not soften their hearts towards him. Exactly how the wounded man was despatched can never now be known. Superintendent Hare gives two of the many varying accounts. Ned Kelly told him that he blew the sergeant's brains out, out of compassion, but then he told Aaron Sherritt, in whose version the superintendent seemed to place more faith, that he made the other desperadoes of the gang fire into the wounded man so that they should be equally guilty of murder with himself, and thereby be prevented from informing against him. Which was correct none but the murderers themselves could say; but examination of the body seemed to bear out Aaron Sherritt's version of the affair. This, when found some days after, was riddled with bullets, and it, as well as Scanlon's, proved how desperate the fight had been. When questioned concerning the murders, Ned Kelly said Kennedy made from tree to tree, firing as he went, and once almost did for him (Kelly). Only almost, however, for poor Kennedy gave his life for his country, and his murderers were left unharmed. His terrible fate sent a thrill of horror through the whole community, and the determination to have the murderers alive or dead took root in the public mind. The sensation caused by this tragedy will be remembered by many yet. It was unparalleled for cold-blooded atrocity in the history of the colony, and the thought of the brave sergeant begging in vain for a brief space of life in which to bid his loved ones good-bye, was for long present in the thoughts of those who had known the ill-fated man. McIntyre escaped, and after many mishaps managed to give the alarm. Had he not done so the fate of the three, to whose memory a handsome monument has been erected at Mansfield by their comrades, might still have been a mystery.

The bushrangers were outlawed, and from that time, knowing they were the lawful prey of any one who could lay hands upon them, they seem to have resolved to prey upon all who came within their reach. A reward of £1,000 was offered for their capture, and no stone left unturned to secure it. Without avail, however. There was much disorganization among the police force of the district, and this could not altogether disappear when Mr. Nicholson, the Assistant Commissioner of Police, was commissioned to take charge of the pursuit, for from that time there were personal feuds and jealousies among the officers which could not fail to have a most demoralising effect upon those under him, as well as minimise the chances of success.

The impression made on the public at the time soon became general, and that the authorities were not prepared to cope with an even less serious emergency was soon evident. The Kellys soon became the theme of every tongue and the dread of every feeling heart. It was almost with a feeling of dread that the newspaper-reading public opened their papers. The usual morbid fascination the details of such crimes exercise over so many human minds was in this case secondary to the terror of apprehension which had seized on the public mind.

By the time the Commission appointed to enquire into the circumstances of the outbreak had realised this, however, and found that Mr. Nicholson had been retarded in his endeavours to do his duty, it was far and away too late to prevent the havoc the Kellys wrought towards the close of their career. The answer of that Commission to Mr. Dixon's protest against their finding in clauses 3 and 5 of the second progress report was—"That there was every reason to believe that Superintendent Hare was in collusion with Captain Standish in the petty and dishonorable persecution to which Mr. Nicholson was subjected for many years whilst honestly endeavouring to discharge his duty to the best of his ability." And to this much of the non-success which attended every effort made for so long must be attributed. This non-success gave rise to much adverse feeling on the part of the community at large. They could not understand it, and being roused to exasperation point by the fiendish malevolence of Ned Kelly towards the wounded and defenceless Sergeant Kennedy, were not slow to give expression to their poor opinion of many of those who sought to bring him to justice. The fate of Kennedy, who was shot into when already wounded to death, made a very profound impression, and even the morbidly sympathetic could find no word to say in the miscreant's defence. This terrible tragedy caused a much needed look into the resources of the police of the district, and in most cases they were found to be wholly inadequate to the need that had arisen. What was discovered to be most necessary was apparently the thorough reorganization and re-arming of the whole force. This, however, was a work of time, and the need of immediate action was most urgent. Even in the short time that had elapsed the outlaws must have had plenty in which to devise and adopt measures for their own safety. Though every effort possible appears to have been put forth by the Government, all was without avail. There seems, too, to have been so much publicity over every move made that the outlaws could have had but little difficulty in keeping themselves acquainted with all that was going on. They were surrounded by friends and sympathisers, never lacking support from their numerous relatives, who looked upon the police as their natural enemies, and regarded outwitting them as the triumphs of life. Against the force of such undisciplined passions, and a knowledge of the country far exceeding their own, the best organised force in the world must have been well nigh powerless. But the police in the Kelly district were far from being this at the time of the outbreak. So it was scarcely surprising that Ned Kelly and his gang enjoyed long immunity from the consequences of their crimes.

Had the officers at the head of affairs generally been on more harmonious terms with each other—more intent on preserving the peace of the country than on their own aggrandisement—the Wombat murders would most probably have been the last, as they were the worst of the criminals' misdeeds. Only two or three days after they occurred the prisoner Williamson, who, it will be remembered, was sentenced with Mrs. Kelly, Skillian, and others, for the attack on Fitzpatrick, gave information that would certainly have led to the speedy arrest of the gang. Though information of such sources is usually received with caution, the police were satisfied of the genuineness of that imparted by the prisoner Williamson. After-effects justified them in this belief. The plan sketched, and the provision log, were found to be as described, but the finding seems to have satisfied those engaged in the pursuit. They went, they saw, but never attempted in this ease to conquer, so the one certain chance to bring the career of the Kellys to an early close was lost for ever. Messrs. Nicholson and Sadlier were severely taken to task for this undeniable neglect of duty by the Commission, but censure was the mildest form of punishment possible for a neglect that caused such loss of life and property. It was known that Mrs. Skillian, one of the Kelly sisters, was very actively engaged, and it was said to be in the work of nightly provisioning the outlaws. The police, however, had apparently too much respect for the sex to interfere in aught that was to their pleasure. So Mrs. Skillian came and went undisturbed on her way. Secure from molestation, the gang went evidently at ease as to their safety. If search parties were at work all round them, numberless friends, and most effectual assistance in the bush telegraph system, with which the gang and so many of their sympathisers were so perfectly acquainted, were at work around them too. That they had much to endure in the way of fatigue and hindrance to their plans is undoubted—the flooding of the Murray the most effectual, and that which drove them back to the fastness from which they came. There was certain proof of their having been seen at Wangaratta, but all those invested with authority in the matter seem to have been alike unfitted to deal with the fact. This bad feeling between Messrs. Standish, Nicholson, and Sadlier made public duty subordinate to personal spleen. Inspector Smith and Sub-Inspector Pewtress proved themselves quite unequal to emergencies, and Sergeant Steele does not appear to have been held blameless for the gang's escape from Wangaratta. That they were there, and in a state of exhaustion that would have made their arrest easy, is undoubted; but from one pair of shoulders to another the responsibility of taking actions was shifted until the gang were again out of reach.

The prisoner Williamson seems to have had no desire to in any way mislead the police, and they verified his statements so far as to make the wonder at their not adopting measures of a more effectual description against the bank robberies that followed, greater. That they were pretty well aware some such attempt was in contemplation is evident. There were many rumors of some such intention, and some from reliable sources, but there was such an utter want of unanimity amongst officers and men that the history of their endeavours to catch the criminals at this period leaves the impression of there having been a series of wild rushes to nowhere particularly defined, which ended about as satisfactorily as they commenced. Mutual recrimination seems to have been that in which most thoroughness, energy, and promptitude was displayed, and in mutual bad feeling among their pursuers lay safety for the gang. These last could not have been ignorant of the state of affairs among their enemies, or of the consequent disorganization. Throughout they seem to have been well acquainted with every move that was to be made, and nearly always to have planned accordingly. Long as it was known that some bank or other in the north-eastern district would be stuck up, yet the sticking-up of that at Euroa came upon all concerned as great a surprise as if there had been no suspicion of any such intended raid. This robbery seems to have been managed in the most cool and systematic way. It was the first on the list of those which were to stamp the Kelly gang as the most daring and resourceful the colony had ever known. One secret of their success was their ability to take their victims in detail more than by surprise, and this must have been the result of a patience and perseverance on the outlaws' part that was certain to command a fairly long run of success. On the part of the pursuers there was a wild rush to horse and arms, hurry and scurry, stir that would have infected a city-full, and in the hush and wildness of the bush townships and settlements must have penetrated easily into haunts where the gang lay concealed. In fact, the sound-carrying capacity of bush and mountain air is so well known to those who have lived in either, that the want of caution displayed by men who must have been well acquainted with such peculiarity, is little short of marvellous. Robbery of one or other of the banks was the contingency which needed most to be guarded against, yet little special effort was made for their protection. Bank officers themselves seem to have been quite inert in the matter; the knowledge that the Kellys might effect a transfer of the property they held in trust to themselves any day did not move them to measures of self protection, nor did the reinforcement of police needed at all the threatened points in the district come to hand. The Commission found afterwards that there was no proof, beyond mere assertions, of such reinforcements having been applied for, and nothing in the evidence to show that either Mr. Nicholson, or Mr. Sadlier realised the danger that was so imminent. So the Kellys had a fair field and everything in their favor.

AUSTRALASIAN
SKETCHER

No. 74.—VOL. VI.   MELBOURNE, SATURDAY, NOVEMBER 23, 1879.   PRICE 6d.

THE BUSHRANGING TRAGEDY : PORTRAITS OF THE FOUR CONSTABLES AND THE TWO KELLYS.

1.—CONSTABLE M'INTYRE.   2.—DONALD KELLY.   3.—CONSTABLE SCANLAN.   4.—SERGEANT KENNEDY.   5.—CONSTABLE M'INTYRE.   6.—DANIEL KELLY.

EUROA BANK ROBBERY

Euroa is a small township situated, as those acquainted with the topography of the land know, a hundred miles or so from the Victorian metropolis, on the Sydney railway line, and the bank which the outlaws chose as the scene of their operations was close to the railway station. As the population of the township numbered some three hundred in all, there is something almost farcical in the ease with which the gang bailed up one after the other of all who came in their way or threatened to impede their progress. The township was quite unprotected; the one repre-sentative of the guardians of the peace it boasted was away, and did not return till the evening, and when he was informed of what had taken place he straightaway took train to Benalla—what to do there deponent knoweth not, for that particular constable is heard of no more. Mr. Nicholson and Mr. Sadlier had been lured to Albury by the report of the outlaws having been seen there the night before the robbery. On the platform at Benalla Mr. Nicholson was informed by Mr. Wyatt, P.M., that telegraphic communication with Melbourne had been destroyed, which did not turn either him or Mr. Sadlier from their purpose. Their suspicions were again aroused at Glenrowan, but the Kellys were evidently in Dame Fortune's good graces, for the two gentlemen sped on to Albury, from whence Mr. Nicholson had immediately to return. The news of the sticking-up reached him about midnight, but all the energy and promptitude evoked by it were of no avail. The outlaws had a good start, and Mr. Nicholson and his search party next day had no success whatever.

By the Euroa Bank robbery the gang profited to the extent of over £2,000 in cash, and a new fit-out from a travelling hawker's van, and rest and refreshment for man and beast at the station—Younghusband's—at which they elected to put up. It was the most convenient point from which to conduct operations, and proved, as the gang pretty well knew it to be, specially adapted for their purposes. About the coolest thing in this was the taking possession of bank manager and family, and driving them to the station, where the other prisoners where whiling away their time as best they might. There was a grim sort of humor in many of Ned Kelly's doings, and it was this element in his nature that won him many a sympathiser. The genuine bushman dearly loves what he calls "a lark," and the genuine bushman and larrikin natures were open books to Ned Kelly. The other members of the gang knew much more of them than was altogether to the profit of the community at large; but to their leader they seemed generally to look for inspiration. The Euroa Bank robbery was as deliberate and daring a deed as could well be committed, and it seems as if there could have been no doubt of the outlaws having been secreted in or near the township for some days previous to the date on which it was committed. This was little less than two months after the Wombat murders had startled the community into the determination to have the murderers—alive or dead. Planning and study only could have enabled the gang to go so systematically about such a business, and to have luck at every turn. They destroyed telegraphic communication, captured and locked up every one who crossed their paths. Superintendent Hare, in a published account of this affair, insists that special measures were taken to protect the Banks, and that all kinds of weapons were supplied to their officers; but if so, measures and weapons were wofully inadequate to the occasion, or else immunity had made those who were to put them in force regard the Kelly scare as a sort of bogey with which to frighten children. No one, at all events, seemed capable of guarding what they held in trust, or to be in any way a match for even one of the gang. The Commission later on, however, decided that there was no proof of any such special effort having been made, and severely blamed Messrs. Nicholson and Sadlier for leaving headquarters at such a time. Of course, after the outlaws had got clear away with their plunder, and the pursuers had been baffled at every turn, there were many hints and insinuations of deliberate activity and practical sympathy for the pursued; but the decision of the Commission *in re* this was:—"A careful scrutiny of the telegrams does not bear out the allegation that the Mansfield contingent were instructed to proceed in a direction opposite to that in which there was a possibility of the gang with their plunder being encountered." So from this suspicion Mr. Nicholson was exonerated. Mr. Pewtress had full power to act as he thought best in the matter, but the result proved that he was not well fitted to decide in regard to it. All efforts to trace the outlaws proved vain. It was about half-past eight before they left the station, after commanding all their prisoners to remain in durance vile for three hours longer; and much as many of these desired to depart at once, they were deterred by the caution of the majority. So it was not until between ten and eleven that the inhabitants got any idea of what had been going on in their midst.

The Euroa Bank robbery, and the coolness and daring with which it was accomplished, will have fixed itself in the minds of many resident now in the colony. That the gang must have been located near the place for some days, or have had very complete information to go upon, was evidenced by the way in which they had all its places and possibilities at their finger ends—the best method, too, of utilising them. From the time of the murders in October to December, the gang had been able to elude all attempts at capture. They had a wide and diversified tract of country, with which they were perfectly well acquainted, in which to select hiding places. They had any number of friends and sympathisers; and the sisters, Mrs. Skillian and Kate Kelly, were as daring as they were devoted to the interests of the gang. Kate Kelly was, according to all accounts, ready to do or dare anything that would lead the police astray or help her brothers, and Mrs. Skillian seemed not to know what fear was. Both were astute enough to keep themselves fairly well out of the clutches of the law, and pretty well unhampered by anything but the surveillance of the police which could not be quite shaken off. The Kelly sympathisers, however, made it of no avail, and to genuine sharpness and activity the gang owed their escape more than once. Their female friends and relations seem never to have been at rest, or to have had the gang out of mind. Provisioning, spying, luring searchers astray—they were ever active and ever useful. Thus the gang could hide as long as they deemed it necessary, confident of supplies, and at leisure to work out their plans. The country was almost inaccessible, except to some hardy and enterprising few, and among these favored few the police evidently were not.

The first step in the Euroa bank robbery was the taking possession of Younghusband's station, which was distant about three miles from the bank. Euroa was a small place, but evidently big enough with promise of profit to tempt the outlaws. The station was, as the latter evidently knew, peculiarly adapted for their purpose—it was a good place from which to conduct operations. Rest and refreshments for man and beast was what the gang demanded on first appearing at Younghusband's station, and the magic name of "The Kelly Gang" ensured its being promptly satisfied. Then a wholesale system of imprisoning came into force.

The station hands were captured as they dropped in one by one, and marched off to the dining—made for the nonce, the detention room. They made little demur when they knew who their captors were, and went into durance vile with a docility that was not the least surprising feature of the affair. By the time the manager of the station, who had been out, returned, most of his employés had been disposed of, and there was no alternative but to "bail up" as desired. Ned Kelly assured him that the gang were not going to take anything, they only wanted food and rest, so Mr. Macauley yielded to the inevitable; he was not imprisoned, nor were any of the women. Ned Kelly seems to have striven ever for the good opinion of the feminine portion of the little crowds he stuck up, and to have impressed some of them very favorably.

He evidently did not regard his assurance of not requiring anything but food and rest as binding in regard of those who came from outside the station. A hawker who came up was relieved of some of his stock, as well as his cart. The outlaws fitted themselves out with clothes from it, as well as with anything that took their fancy. Up to this time they had met nothing in the shape of resistance; but the obstinacy of the hawker, whose goods were so disposed of, tried the always easily roused tempers of the gang. The efforts of the manager, however, prevented the bloodshed which would most probably have been the prelude to more. Dan Kelly, who seems throughout to have been the most uncontrollable of the gang, was eager for the fray, but Ned Kelly allowed himself to be persuaded, and the hawker was permitted to go unharmed to join the other prisoners.

The next addition to the number of prisoners was a party of four who had been shooting in the Strathbogie Ranges. Had they not been taken by surprise there might have been a different tale than this to tell, for they seem to have resented their capture and to have been unwilling to give in. Ned Kelly confronted them as they were entering the station gates, and accused one of them of being Ned Kelly. "You have stolen that spring cart," he said. But they asserted that they had not done so, and were all honest men. This Kelly pretended not to believe, and produced a pair of handcuffs, making as if to put them on. The party thought then that he was a policeman. The one who had been riding came up, and when he was told that the station was stuck-up wanted to get into the cart and load the guns, not knowing that he was proposing it before the man who had done the deed. Kelly advised him not to do so, and it was not till they reached the station that the party became aware of who their captors were. The shooting party soon swelled the number of the imprisoned band. There was over twenty men who were thus rendered *hors de combat* by the determination and daring of four men only.

From the sticking-up of the station the gang seem to have gone most systematically to work. They destroyed all chance of telegraphic communication, captured and imprisoned all who came in their way and were likely to interfere with their plans. Having thus made all safe, they started for the National Bank at Euroa. Those honest folks to whom the carts belonged had the doubtful pleasure of seeing them taken for the avowed purpose of conveyance of stolen bank treasure, and of knowing that they were powerless to prevent the proposed depletion. The gang seem to have had no fear of being unsuccessful, and made their plans with a deliberation and even jocularity, which bespoke a certainty of success. One remained behind to guard the prisoners and against the possibility of an alarm being given. It was one against twenty; but the chances were all in favor of the one, and Joe Byrne seems to have kept the whole of them in complete subjection during the temporary absence of the rest of the gang.

Access to the bank was obtained by means of a small cheque, which Mr. Macauley was forced to sign; and while Ned Kelly was parleying with the clark the other man effected an entrance at the back. As usual, the first step was to take possession of the firearms. Then the manager was bailed up in his office; he was soon made to see that resistance was vain, and the money of the bank go into the outlaws' possession. There was not enough to satisfy Ned Kelly, who evidently knew as much of the bank's resources as the manager himself, and, by dint of threats and determination, Kelly forced them to yield up the rest, getting over £2,000 in cash and a quantity of gold dust. He then carried off the whole family, as well as the servants, to the station, which must by that time have been pretty well crowded out.

Mrs. Scott, who was evidently of a blithe and fearless nature, seems to have done much to keep Ned Kelly in good humor, and no harm came to the numerous family that had to join the procession back to the station. Mr. Scott does not appear to have been easily induced to do anything that might assist the gang in their operations; but Ned Kelly, who was evidently in a genial frame of mind, did not press him to far, so all was kept smooth. The journey to the station was accomplished without let or hindrance, and Mrs. Scott was a decided acquisition to the company there. On the journey Ned Kelly was very communicative. He seemed to seize on every opportunity to parade his deeds, and reasons for them. That there was no foundatrion for many of them is certain, and those who listened believed just as much of what was said as pleased them. The watch taken from the ill-fated Kenedy was exhibited on every possible occasion, and the ruffians openly exulted over the commotion they had caused among the police.

A train came up near the station after the gang had returned to it, but never a signal dared the prisoners make, so it passed on after a time, those in it quite unconscious of what was going on within a short distance of them. When the train had departed the gang completed their preparations for leaving the station. When they were ready to depart Ned Kelly warned the prisoners that they were not to attempt to escape for a given time, and although some were desirous of doing so as soon as they thought the coast was clear they were over-ruled; the spell of the Kelly gang was potent enough to keep more than four times their number obedient to its will. Fear of a repetition of the Wombat tragedy seems to have paralysed most people with whom the gang came in contact. The gang had shown to what lengths they could go, and this, together with the presence of women and children among the prisoners, must have often kept the men of doing anything that might cause bloodshed.

Though there was some geniality and social pleasure among the prisoners, there must also have been much anxiety and suspense, for the temper of the gang was known to be uncertain. Their lives were already forfeit, and no worse fate than this could befall them for any additional misdeeds; hence it must have been with a feeling of considerable relief that the departure of the gang was watched. After this exploit the gang disappeared as completely as if the earth had swallowed them up. There were rumors and reports innumerable of their having been seen at various places, but they were never seen by those whose business it was to catch them.

When the imprisoned ones at Younghusband's station decided to venture out, the inhabitants of the town were still in blissful unconsciousness of all that had happened. Mr. Scott found everything just as he had been compelled to leave it, and there was nothing whatever to make any one anticipate that sensation that was in store for the colony of Victoria generally, which was that the marauders should get off scot free with their plunder. The impassable and impenetrable nature of what was, and indeed still is, called "the Kelly Country," formed a barrier which there was no getting over in order to make their pursuit successful. Nature seemed to favor the outlaws in every possible way, added to which they had been well acquainted with the peculiarities and fastness of the whole district long before they had had to flee for their lives. Every boulder, mountain spur, and ravine was familiar to them, and the way in which they found their way through the almost impenetrable scrub was little short of marvellous.

The Euroa fiasco made some little change among pursuers as well as the method of pursuit. Mr. Nicholson was recalled, and his enemies were not slow to impute as the reason motives derogatory to his credit. There was evidently much painful feeling, and Mr. Nicholson must have felt most deeply his being superseded at such a period; it was true his health had given way a little, consequent on the excessive strain on his energies, but the Commission were afterwards fully satisfied that there was something in the nature of a conspiracy against this officer, and much long-continued underhand work. This, however, was not known at the time, and Mr. Nicholson had to relinguish the pursuit, and with it the hope of added prestige and promised reward. In the month's grace accorded he endeavored to the utmost of his ability to bring the outlaws to justice, but without avail, and, consequently, had to retire in favor of Superintendent Hare, who thus reaped the benefit of what the Commission afterwards characterized as "the petty and dishonorable persecution to which Mr. Nicholson had been subjected for many years."

Superintendent Hare was apparently not satisfied with his triumph, for he sought in his official report to further prejudice the authorities against the retiring Assistant Commissioner of Police by asserting that Mr. Nicholson would give him no verbal information whatever. This officer was subsequently exonerated from that as from many other more petty charges when the Commission of Enquiry sent in its report, for throughout the whole course of events it would seem as if he had been the victim of circumstances and *malice prepense* on the part of many who should have aided him rather than added to his disability, and that to that fact more than anything else failure was due.

Superintendent Hare and Captain Standish were now in charge of the pursuit, and a great deal of activity, in much of which there was zeal without discretion, prevailed. Almost their first step—the enforcement of the Felons Apprehension Act—provoked hostility of a widespread character. Under it a number of people suspected of practically sympathising with the gang were arrested, but in nearly all cases suspicion proved to be misdirected, as nothing could be brought forward in the way of evidence to support them; hence, after a wearisome delay and periodical reappearances at the Court, the whole lot were discharged, and returned to swell the number of the real and more active sympathisers of the gang, who must have been laughing to their sleeves at such fruitless and arbitrary proceedings. It was actions such as these that brought the police into contempt in the district—arresting people on suspicion for which not a shadow of proof was forthcoming. The hastiness of all proceedings at this period could not have been in any way calculated to enhance the majesty of the law. There was apparently a want of deliberation and a general hotheadedness displayed at times which was about the last thing to have been expected from a force officered by men who for years had been in authority in the service. The gang of outlaws were, it was known, concealed in the ranges, but the police were quite unable to trace them. Veritable will-o'-the-wisps did the outlaws prove at this time. Their system of communication was so perfect that they were always able to get safely into another place of refuge ere the police could carry out their intention to search the one in which they were known to have been.

From that time until February, 1879, when the next bank robbery took place, the gang abode wherever it suited them. They had several mountain retreats to choose from, and the Warby Ranges, the Woolshed (near Sebastopol), and the neighbourhood of the King River were each in turn honored (?) with their presence. At this time a detachment of the garrison artillery were sent into the district for the protection of the townships in which further bank robberies might be looked for, and later on these artillery were reinforced by others. The four men pursued, however, managed to keep out of the clutches of those who with all their superiority in numbers, training and arms, were vastly inferior in what was far more essential for their success than any other gift, viz., bush-craft. All the tricks resorted to and ingenuity displayed by the pursuers were of no avail against the knowledge of the whole district possessed by the pursued. Superintendent Hare had now a force available large enough for all purposes of pursuit, and the hardships endured by his men, added to the costs incurred by the Government, must have been a *bonne bouche* for the outlaws whenever they reflected upon it. If these latter had also something in the way of hardships to endure they were peculiarly fitted to endure them, for were they not as hardy as they were daring and cruel?

SUPERINTENDENT HARE

When Superintendent Hare had mastered all the details of his predecessor's plans of working, and varied them to suit his own ideas of what was needed for success, he proceeded to introduce some fresh ones. A cave party was formed, in which Aaron Sherritt, the great friend and ally of the Kelly gang, was included. This Sherritt seems to have been much sought after for purposes of the pursuit. Though young in years, and apparently endowed with every physical power that would have enabled him to live a life worth living, he preferred that in which there was not only more risk than reward, but full play of all the evil tendencies of human nature. He seems to have been hardy and courageous to a degree, not by any means ill-looking, and to have been somewhat popular among the lawless crowd with whom he worked for so long. To the Kelly gang Aaron Sherritt was for many months an invaluable friend and ally. He was what was called a "bush telegraph," and, according to all accounts, was unequalled in that capacity. He was so thoroughly acquainted with all the movements of the gang, and so conversant with their methods, that Superintendent Hare considered he had reason to congratulate himself when Aaron came over to aid the cause of law and order. The Superintendent had great faith in the honesty of Aaron's intentions, and was confident, too, that neither the gang or their sympathisers suspected the intended treachery of their trusted friend and "bush telegraph." If, however, this was the case, it seems strange that no success whatever attended any of the movements suggested by Aaron. He eventually appears to have convinced others beside Superintendent Hare of his fidelity to the police, but if those he was seeking to betray had no suspicion of his intended treachery to themselves they managed to elude his vigilance. That Aaron had a knowledge of the country equal to that of the outlaws themselves is undoubted, and, up to the time of going over to the side of the police, so complete an acquaintance with the outlaws' movements that it seems as if they could not have escaped unless they had had very strong suspicions of his honesty of purpose in regard to themselves.

From the time he began the work with the police he seemed in some way to lose the run of the gang. True, he was able to furnish forth information occasionally for which there seemed good foundation, and the reader is more than once forced to the conclusion that Aaron himself was once or twice purposely misled by the gang or their friends. He was led into the belief that Goulburn would be the scene of the outlaws' next bank exploit, and while a good deal of attention was being centred on this idea the gang took literal possession of Jerilderie, New South Wales, between fifty and sixty miles from the Murray. Then Aaron was induced to attend the Whorouly races in the hope of meeting Joe Byrne. Needless to say the later did not appear. Either the gang had taken alarm at something and altered their plans, or faith in their former ally was not as perfect as it had been. If, as Aaron Sherritt averred, Joe Byrne and Dan Kelly had been with him a few days before he fell in with Superintendent Hare, endeavouring to get him to join in an intended raid on the Goulburn Bank, it would be interesting to know what took place between the three. There seems little doubt of the outlaws having been seen at the time and place mentioned, added to which the fact of Aaron Sherritt having from that time thrown in his lot with the police, points to something in the nature of a disagreement between the three scoundrels, for Aaron Sherritt was very little superior in nature to any of the gang. In fact, in spite of the sympathy which all must feel at a man in full health and strength being as suddenly done to death as Aaron Sherritt was, yet the thought of the intended betrayal of old friends and schoolfellows must in this case largely nullify it. It is possible to condone treachery when it is the outcome of sudden passion or revengeful feeling, but the thought of betraying erring humanity for monetary considerations has ever been repugnant to the human soul. Various reasons have been assigned for Aaron Sherritt's secession from his former friends, but there is nothing either in his life or actions to show that anything but pecuniary considerations influenced him. These would-be captors, however, were powerless to command success, and on the 10th February, 1879, the gang again made another successful raid.

This was the date on which the Jerilderie Bank robbery took place, and the manner and method of its committal must have been something of a shock to nineteen century belief in the efficacy of law-enforcing power.

This is the document given to me by Ned Kelly when the Bank at Jerilderie was stuck-up in Feby 1879

JERILDERIE BANK ROBBERY

That a township containing upwards of three hundred people, and boasting a police station and two constables invested with all the powers and authority to make such a feat impossible, had simply to allow the bank to be relieved of its funds as if no such safeguards had been in existence passes belief. The sticking up of the Jerilderie Bank reads like a romance. In fact, were any one asked to believe such a robbery possible, even in the olden times, they would most probably decline to do so. They might credit the fact of three hundred people being able to render four bushrangers *hors de combat*, but that of this number of determined men setting the large number at defiance, as the Kelly gang did at Jerilderie, would seem more than incredible. Yet they accomplished this, and with a coolness and ease

that is not the least astonishing feature in the affair. The method and daring displayed in the raid on Jerilderie proves that the outlaws were men of no mean intelligence and ability, and makes greater the pity of such strong and resourceful natures being turned to evil instead of good.

The constables were lured out of their beds and into their intended captors' presence by the report of some trouble in the township, and were soon completely at their mercy. None could more thoroughly appreciate the reversing of the usual order of things in regard to the police that the outlaws themselves, and there must have been grim enjoyment of the joke of turning the key on the unfortunate constables at Jerilderie, among them.

The Sunday passed without any suspicion being excited, and the gang seem to have made themselves as generally agreeable and comfortable as possible. They disguised themselves as policemen, and compelled one of the imprisoned constables to go with them on reconnoitreing expedition. During this they no doubt perfected plans for the next day's work.

On the Monday the fun, which was all on one side, commenced. They took possession of the Royal Hotel, and one after another of its customers or visitors were captured and imprisoned. All in the hotel were treated likewise, but the general population of the township seem to have been quite unaware of what was going forward. Having cleared the way for their great task—the robbing of the bank—the outlaws set to work. The accountant was the first bailed up, the sub-accountant soon shared a similar fate, which both felt to be a particularly hard one when it devolved upon them to find their manager, who was to be taken into custody also, so Mr. Jarleton soon formed one of the procession. On the return to the bank all the cash available—upwards of £2,000—was appropriated, one or two prisoners made, and some of the books and documents belonging to the bank burned or destroyed.

The next additions to the number of those imprisoned at the hotel were the telegraph clerks. The wires were then cut and the insulators destroyed; the gang thereby insured themselves against pursuit for at least time enough to get clear away with their booty. Time was everything, and the systematic way in which the whole affair was managed contributed more to its success that any daring that was displayed. It would have been matter for surprise had such an evidently well thought out plan miscarried. Of course the gang got clear away. They had a good start, untiring energy, and that promptitude of thought and action, which is often akin to genius.

The Jerilderie Bank robbery was as complete a surprise as the gang's other exploits had been. They had kept so out of the way, and comparatively quiet, while they had assumedly been living on the proceeds of their last robbery, that fear of them seems to have died away a little. Though they were settled in the threatened districts many who would not have been greatly surprised by a visit from the Kellys, yet there were few who were in any way adequately prepared to receive them, or seriously anticipated having to do so. Once the nine days' wonder and sensation was over, each resident seems to have dropped into the way of regarding the possible visit of the gang as a rather remote contingency, and to speculate who or what town would be stuck-up next, instead of being themselves prepared for a possible surprise.

The gang did not signalise themselves further until February, when the Jerilderie Bank was robbed, except by consistently baffling their pursuers. They were generally supposed to be in Victoria, though report continued to credit them with the intention of soon making an appearance in some part of another New South Wales. Even Aaron Sherritt was unable to discover which. He and those with whom he worked fixed their suspicions on Goulburn, having reason to believe that the bank there would be the next favored with a visit; which suspicion, no doubt, had something to do with the ease with which the Jerilderie Bank robbery was managed. Jerilderie, like Euroa, is a small town, but quite large enough for what the outlaws required. It is in New South Wales, and its people seem to have as little anticipated a visit from the dreaded gang as even they could wish. As before mentioned, the two constables stationed there were roused from sleep by the report of some trouble in the township. They came out at once, and while talking to Ned Kelly were bailed up, and being undressed and unarmed were powerless to help either themselves or give the alarm to others. The constable's wife and family were withheld from making known how matters stood by the threat of the imprisoned constables being shot if they did; and then the outlaws proceeded to avail themselves of the comforts and conveniences provided by Government to facilitate proceedings in regard to such as themselves.

THE GANG'S COOL DARING

The constable's wife was made to go through her accustomed duties next day, so that suspicion should not be excited, but she was most carefully watched. The members of the gang disguised themselves as policemen, and made the constables take them out, and make them acquainted with the various points of interest to them. The next day, too, the constable had the doubtful pleasure of introducing the leader of the gang at the hotel, which he had decided was the best for their purpose. Before the name of Ned Kelly all seemed to go down, and all that he wanted was soon at his command. He coolly announced his intention of robbing the bank, and set about it in the systematic manner which had insured him success in his previous undertakings. As at Euroa, so in this instance—all who came near where the outlaws were located were captured an imprisoned. Constable Devine and his family had been safely locked up before the gang left the police station, hence there was no possibility of alarm being given. Leaving the Station unguarded by any of the gang seemed to denote a pretty thorough acquaintance with the resources and habits of the township.

The Bank of New South Wales was then the point of interest for them. This they entered boldly. Their confidence in themselves was not to be shaken, and the coolness with which man after man, little less brave or determined than themselves, was bailed up certainly was something astonishing. They were, however, armed only by nature. Man's ingenuity had furnished the gang with weapons that made nature's gifts of health, strength, and intelligence, of little avail. The accountant and sub-accountant of the bank were made to surrender at discretion. The manager was in his bath, and as helpless as everybody else was destined to be that day, but was soon brought to understand what had happened and the uselessness of resistance. The accountant was then made to hand over what cash he had at hand; but this did not satisfy Ned Kelly, who was evidently aware that there was more available, for he persisted in his demand for more until all was in his possession. It says something for the courage of those who had it in charge that they were able to make even so brief a stand against the bloodthirsty leader of such a gang. When he had got all—upwards of £2,000 in cash, a quantity of gold dust, and satisfied himself with bank books and documents—a further capture was made! A Justice of the Peace and the proprietor of the local paper were bailed up, but the representative of the Fourth Estate proved that he knew how to use his heels as well as his head, and made good his escape. The reader of various and varying accounts of this sensational affair will naturally wonder how it was that no alarm was given by this newspaper genius, Mr. Gill, for had he had his wits about him the robbers might not have got off as easily as they did; but the spell of the Kelly gang was over all. It seems to have been common sense rather than courage that was paralysed in most instances. Search was made for Mr. Gill, but without success, Ned Kelly's motive being apparently the publication of a sketch of his life. How confident he felt of eluding capture was evidenced by his saying to the accountant of the bank, who had been compelled to accompany him in the search, and promised to get the sketch published—"Get it printed; I have not had time to finish it, but will complete it later on; 'tis a bit of my life."

NED KELLY AS AN AUTHOR

One can imagine with what eagerness that sketch was afterwards opened and perused. It, however, proved in nowise different to the oral sketches with which Ned Kelly was in the habit of favoring his captured audiences. He was, of course, a victim to police malevolence, that goes without saying with gentlemen of Mr. Ned Kelly's stamp. He had apparently been in trouble from a child. His first sentence of imprisonment was when he was only fourteen years old, and from that time up to the period when his name and doings became the sensation of the colonies, he was in all the trouble that violent and undisciplined natures make for themselves and others. Unchecked criminal tendencies seemed to have kept him in a continual broil with the police, but in spite of all the charges he brought against them they seem to have acted with leniency rather than malevolence towards him. The most tangible grievance Ned Kelly had was that against Fitzpatrick, and the way the ground of complaint was shifted from "attempt to arrest an innocent brother" to alleged insult to a sister, and, again, to persecution of the mother who had "seen better days," and who had, her son asserted, been convicted on Fitzpatrick's testimony, show that the constable was used as a convenient scapegoat rather than anything else, when the criminal tendencies of the family made such necessary. This constable was afterwards dismissed from the force, but it was for general unfitness for duty, not the Kelly affair in particular, though, of course, that had a good deal to do with it. Superintendent Hare, however, said that Ned Kelly had admitted there was no truth whatever in the accusations in question.

In the autobiographical sketch of Ned Kelly, the only part published was that relating to the Wombat murders, and this added only to the feeling against the outlaws instead of rousing the public sympathy which the writer had hoped for. There was some faint feeling for the murderers while there was an impression abroad that the murdered constables had in some measure brought their fate on themselves, but when it was known that they were deliberately shot down the last trace of this sympathy vanished. Ned Kelly said that Kennedy was killed in "a fair stand-up fight," but how there could be anything fair in the attack of four against one it is difficult to conjecture. It was cowardly, wanton, cruel in the extreme, and should for all time dissipate the thought that there was anything like true bravery or heroism in the gang which could be guilty of such a deed.

Ned Kelly having unburdened his soul in this manuscript, and eased his mind by compelling this promise to publish the same, was able to turn his attention to matters that were to them of more pecuniary importance. Before leaving Jerilderie the gang appropriated everything they took a fancy to, and the fear of harm coming to those imprisoned must have been strong indeed when Dan Kelly and Hart could with impunity, as according to all accounts they did, riot through the streets of the captured township celebrating their victory by all sorts of braggadocio, even after the chief members of the gang had departed. Though but a few hours elapsed before the alarm was given, and every endeavor possible was made to instantly secure them, the robbers got clear off with their plunder apparently without the last trouble.

New South Wales and Victoria, united by their common misfortune, were stirred into such joint action that the wonder is how they managed to so fail in all their endeavours to trace them. The power and the dread of the Kelly gang, however, was so great that even the reward of £8,000, to which it was increased after the Jerilderie affair became known, was powerless to make prudence yield to cupidity. All sections of the community were astir. Many of the lower classes openly gloried in what they deemed the heroism of their kind, but the majority began to feel with the more law-abiding section of the community that the sooner the rascals were brought to justice the better it would be for all concerned. That they had got back into some of their Victorian retreats was pretty well known, but though the authorities on both sides of the Border were equally active, and furnished the papers with "copy" to an extent that must have smoothed many an editorial brow, they achieved no other success. The papers of the time teem with "The Kellys," and they teem too with much that must have caused the gang and their friends to chuckle. There seems to have been altogether too much publicity over measures to be adopted for their capture. It was by this time known throughout the colonies that the gang had means of becoming speedily acquainted with any move that was to be made, yet the precautions taken against this could not be regarded as in any way adequate unless there was a certainty of the Kellys and their friends being unable to read the newspapers. There were certainly many of them as ignorant as they were criminally inclined; at the same time there were many well educated and otherwise superior people who were from inclination or perforce Kelly sympathisers, and from these much knowledge of precautionary or offensive measures must have been gained by the gang.

The bank robbery at Jerilderie proved that the gang were in earnest in the line of life they had taken up, and it could have been small consolation to the section of the public robbed to know that it was their own money that was being used to keep justice at bay. The robbers were now supplied for a while, and while their money lasted no doubt felt that all was right. The robbery was more than a nine days' wonder, and the government resources of two colonies proved unequal to the task of bringing to justice four young men who had elected to defy it and all the law could impose.

Before leaving Jerilderie Ned Kelly as usual tried to pose as a martyr to police vindictiveness and a hero to boot, but much of what he said was known to be untrue, so that it had little effect. Even when those disposed to make a hero of him were inclined to regard him most kindly they were conscious of meanness, of lying, and inordinate vanity that helped to reveal the clay feet of their idol, and left a sense of disgust which is never possible when dwelling in thought on the truly heroic. How any one could see aught approaching to heroism in any of the Kelly gang it is impossible to understand. Their thoughts, language, and pursuits were vile—they seemed to revel in all that was lowest in human nature, and at no time, even in their tragic ends, did there seem to be anything approaching to nobility. There are redeeming qualities in most men's lives, but it has not yet been made apparent what the redeeming quality in those of Kelly gang could be.

The commencement of the trouble—the shooting at Fitzpatrick—appears to have been the least criminal of all their acts, for it was done more in the scuffle and heat of passion than anything that occurred after. There is no doubt, too, that Fitzpatrick's personal unpopularity had something to do with provoking this. A little tact and judgment displayed in the execution of his task among such people might have averted the outbreak, which was precipitated by the attempt to arrest Dan Kelly. Though many reasons have been given for the attack upon Fitzpatrick, there is nothing whatever in any of the evidence given to justify any but that of vindictive hatred for the force in general, and for these numbers of it in particular who contrived to make themselves as unpopular as the rules they had to enforce. Fitzpatrick seems to have been one of these last, and to have been successful in opening the floodgates of passion which was to cause such loss of life and such an enormous expenditure of money.

In the Fitzpatrick affair, which took place apparently in a fury of passion, there was something to extenuate, but the Wombat murders were so fiendishly deliberate, so wantonly cruel, that even the most tender-hearted of those who always feel for the criminal could find no word to say on their behalf. It is difficult, indeed, to see how even the greatest glorifier of evil could find anything in Ned Kelly's career over which to exult.

After the Jerilderie bank robbery there was commotion in both colonies. The rewards offered by Victoria and New South Wales, added to what was offered by the banks, mounted up to the substantial total of £8,000, and none had greater hopes of getting the lion's share than Aaron Sherritt and Superintendent Hare. This last officer proved most active in his endeavours after this—in fact, his general vigor of purpose and action met with some commendation afterwards. Captain Standish does not seem to have been in any way so inclined, and here again we have the commanding officers of the pursuit somewhat at odds with each other. Whether Superintendent Hare's usefulness and energy was in any way damped by the general apathy of his chief is not known, but it is certain that it had an enervating effect on other officers, who seem to have been completely blocked at times by their unapproachable Chief Commissioner.

It was in human nature perhaps to weary sometimes of the subject, but duty to the country should have dominated human nature in such a case. Be this as it may, however, it did not apparently dominate the Chief Commissioner at any time, and so there was the feeling of a grievance between officers and men which could not in any way advance the interests of pursuit.

This, although it was still being actively prosecuted, was as yet barren of results. It was known that the gang had made a return to their Victorian haunts after the Jerilderie bank robbery, but it was not known whether they had remained in any of them. There were plenty of appearances reported. Spook-like they appeared and disappeared. Sometimes, perhaps, the wish in certain minds would be father to the thought, and the police be sent off on a wild goose chase; but for some reports there was sufficient foundation to justify steps being taken. With no result, however, and Captain Standish and Superintendent Hare returned to Melbourne with little more gains for their pains than had fallen to Mr. Nicolson's lot.

V.   R.

MURDER
OF
POLICE.
£2,500 REWARD

WHEREAS, by a notice published in the *Government Gazette* bearing date the 30th October 1878, a Reward of **FIVE HUNDRED POUNDS** was offered by the Government for such information as would lead to the capture of each of the four men therein described charged with the murder of certain members of the Police Force, in the **King River** District: **AND WHEREAS** it is decided to increase the Reward for the apprehension of one of the said four offenders, named **EDWARD KELLY,** from **FIVE HUNDRED POUNDS** to **ONE THOUSAND POUNDS: NOTICE IS HEREBY GIVEN** that a Reward of **ONE THOUSAND POUNDS** will be paid by the Government for such information as will lead to the capture of the said **EDWARD KELLY** and **FIVE HUNDRED POUNDS** for each of the other three offenders referred to in the said notice of 30th October last.

This notification is in lieu of that of the 30th day of October 1878 above referred to, which is hereby cancelled.

GRAHAM BERRY,
Chief Secretary.

Chief Secretary's Office,
Melbourne, 13th December 1878.

BY AUTHORITY: JOHN FERRES, GOVERNMENT PRINTER, MELBOURNE.

EMPLOYMENT OF BLACK TRACKERS

The next move was the employment of black trackers. Their services had been offered in 1878 by Mr. D. T. Seymour, the then Queensland Commissioner, but Captain Standish had refused to entertain the idea. After the Jerilderie trouble and failure on the part of the police, however, it was evident some new move must be made, so Captain Standish was induced to consent to the employment of the services of black trackers. From the first, however, the contempt in which their powers seem to have been held by him caused a latent feeling of bitterness. For some time the relations between the officers of the respective forces were cordial enough, but Captain Standish was destined to dissension. Although he conceded to the wish for black trackers, he would not give their commanding officer the right to work them according to his own ideas and experience of their methods and capabilities. Furthermore, Captain Standish expressed his opinion of their general unfitness for the work to be done with a freedom that was calculated to give rise to much wounded feeling. The officers who were in active charge of the pursuit, and were well able to judge, spoke in highly favourable terms of their powers and usefulness, but Captain Standish was not to be convinced, and want of harmony was again the most retarding influence.

The Commission of Enquiry found that in "witholding information from the officers in charge of the trackers on one occasion, and by making Superintendent Hare a party to the trans-action, Captain Standish adopted the most effectual means of sowing discord among the officers." Discord means failure in nearly all cases, and more particularly in such difficult ones as these. His behaviour to Mr. O'Connor was in every way lacking in courtesy, and as this last gentleman was a stranger to the country he was endeavoring to serve, such conduct was the more reprehensible on Captain Standish's part. It is not surprising, therefore, that more in the way of success had not attended the pursuit. Those in charge could not pull together, and those under them were bound to be in every way affected by any such failure. Inspector Brook Smith came in for more censure than others for his inactivity when in pursuit, and for negligence and incapacity when the one most certain chance of capturing the gang that occurred throughout presented itself.

Constable King, Stanhope O'Connor, Queensland black trackers, Superintendent Sadlier and Commissioner Standish; at Benalla.

MR. NICHOLSON
RESUMES CHARGE

Captain Standish and Superintendent Hare having failed to accomplish anything more than their predecessors, it remained for Mr. Nicholson, who then resumed charge of the pursuit, to see what he could do in the matter. The difficulties this officer labored under have been referred to before. They increased rather than lessened as time went on, so that what he achieved was really as much to his credit as if success had attended his efforts. His usefulness was retarded and his energies crippled by the never ceasing persecution to which he was subjected; and, furthermore, as he was not given *carte blanche* in regard to expenditure, he had no such opportunities for distinguishing himself as Captain Standish had enjoyed.

Retrenchment seems to have become as all-pervading an idea with the Government than as it is now. Mr. Nicholson's resumption of the charge of pursuit was marked by an expressed desire for reduction in expenses. Though the danger from the outlaws was as great as it had been at any previous time, yet so pressing was the desire for retrenchment that reductions were gradually effected. That this did not give Mr. Nicholson as fair a chance as others had had before him is certain. He had to pay many expenses out of his own pocket, and, though they were always refunded, yet the knowledge of having to do with less when more was urgently required must have narrowed him in plans as well as pocket. The garrison artillery were withdrawn by degrees, and reductions made in the strength of the police force. Mr. Nicholson had to do with a considerably smaller number of men and much less money, and on applying for additional men for ordinary duty had some sent who were utterly useless for the purpose required.

Nothing in the whole Kelly trouble seems so astonishing as the way in which crime was allowed to grow in such a district. It was not as if those in authority could be ignorant of the inevitable consequences of an aggregation of scoundrelism. The Lloyds, the Kellys, the Quins, and the kindred spirits which each drew around them, were all well known to the police from the first, and at the start might surely have been dealt with in some such way as to have made the outbreak furnished forth in this history an impossibility. The tract of country—in a sense bounded by the townships of Benalla, Beechworth, and Mansfield, and that which stretched away west of the railway line to the Murray— was one seething mass of crime and trouble long before the doings of the Kelly gang rendered it more infamous still.

The police of the district were well acquainted with those phases of human nature by which they were surrounded. There were, too, men who knew by experience how crime progress by leaps and bounds when such families as the Kellys, Quins, and Lloyds intermarry and settle down within hall of each other. No constable in the district could plead ignorance of the threatening state of affairs, or that he could not form some idea of what such close connections must culminate in. The urgent need for the Glenmore station was well know long before it was established, and it was never needed more than at the time the Government elected to abolish it. It had certainly been the means of greatly mitigating the evil that for so long had been rampant, and finally drove the elder Quin, who was at that period the head and front of the general offending, out of district.

Now it seems as if the authorities, who knew so well what Quin and his family were, should have known also that driving them into another district, without taking steps to keep them, or have them kept under the same strict surveillance, was the surest way of spreading the evil. When the Quins moved the law should have moved with them. It would not have cost a quarter as much in money and life to worry such a lot out of the country altogether as it did to hunt down the Kelly Gang. Instead of the espionage and extra safeguards that ought to have been established, however, the Quins' departure from Glenmore seems to have been the signal for the relaxing of many of them.

"In the opinion of your Commissioners," reads the report of the Commission, "the abolition of the Glenmore station, the reduction in the numerical strength of the force, and the substitution of inferior and inexperienced constables for those more competent, necessarily weakened that effective and complete police surveillance without which the criminal classes in all countries become more and more restive and defiant of authority." This was putting it very mildly when we consider what this laxity had brought about—the Wombat murders, the sticking-up of the Euroa and Jerilderie Banks, and the state of perpetual terror in which for years so many of the community were kept. The murder of Sergeant Kennedy alone was enough to have made the censure more scathing, for nothing made a greater impression on the public.

Thus there was a great accumulation of wrong to be dealt with when Mr. Nicholson resumed charge of the pursuit, this time with strong hopes of success, but under conditions that were scarcely favourable thereto. There was as much feeling at that time against the force as for it. So many of those in authority had been found wanting that all confidence in the force had vanished. Superintendent Sadleir—who initiated what is known as the "Sebastopol charge," which according to evidence before the Commission, "could have been heard a mile off," and in which, it was affirmed, "everything was done as though it were desirable to give the gang, supposing they were in the neighborhood, timely warning of the approach of the police"—showed such want of judgment that when the time for enquiry came he was, on the recommendation of the Commission, placed at the bottom of the list of all the superintendents.

Inspector Brook Smith made even a worse mess of his command, and the Commission could find no words too severe for the result of what they decided was indolence as well as incompetence. They considered that a most favorable opportunity of capturing the outlaws at a very early period in their career of crime—namely, on November 4th, 1878—was lost owing to the incompetence and indolence of Inspector Brook Smith. That his conduct in not starting in pursuit of the outlaws immediately on receiving information of their having been seen passing under the bridge at Wangaratta, and in not having properly followed up the tracks of the outlaws in the Warby Ranges, merited dismissal from the force. The memory of former services made the Commission refrain from this extreme step, so they recommended that he be called on to retire from the service on a pension of £100 a year, which was punishment enough for one who must often have hoped for a very different ending to his public career. Sergeant Steele was also held responsible for the failure to capture on this occasion, as he had full power to act on his own discretion, and by doing so would have prevented the loss of life and enormous expenditure of money incurred subsequently in the extermination of the outlaws.

There was apparently incompetence all round. From their position in the force it is to be assumed this could not be very generally brought against Captain Standish and Superintendent Hare, but if more competent they were not more successful in bringing the outlaws' career to a speedy close than those who had preceded or were working under them. Sub-Inspector Pewtress was the wrong man in the wrong place, and if Mr.Nicholson was fitted to occupy his position then the difficulties and the cloud under which he labored must have preventing him proving it. Thus, unfortunate in the way it was officered, what could have been expected from the pursuit but that which for years was its result? A long and almost uninterfered-with career of crime for the outlaws, and a physically and financially exhausting pursuit for those who had to enforce law and order.

The tactics of the Assistant-Commissioner of Police, Mr. Nicholson, on resuming charge will be more comprehensible in his own words:—"All things were on a different basis owing to reduction in expenses, numerical strength, and decided inferiority in men placed at my disposal, and the steps I took to make all as effectual as possible are briefly these:—"I set to and re-organised the men on this basis, and adopted the view that with the materials at my command the best course to adopt would be to secure places from outrage where there was treasure, so that the outlaws would be baffled in any attempt to replenish their coffers. I stationed a small body of men at Wodonga, under Sergeant Harkin; another at Wangaratta, under Sergeant Steele; another at Bright, under Senior-Constable Shoebridge; and also at Mansfield, under Sub-Inspectors Toohey and Pewtress. At each of these there was barely strength enough for a search party, but they could make up a fair party—seven or eight—by calling in men from neighboring stations. The only place were a complete search party was kept was at Benalla. I instructed the police throughout the district to arrange to get quietly from two to four townsmen of the right sort, who would turn out, and aid in case of attack." All, however, without avail, for it was September, 1879, before anything like positive information was forthcoming; then news of the gang having been seen at Wangaratta was conveyed to Mr. Nicholson, who considered it sufficiently reliable to act upon. A search party was quickly assembled; but, alas! again masterly inactivity became the order of the day. Mr. Sadleir's knowledge did not seem certain enough to Mr. Nicholson to warrant the intended search being proceeded with, and it was abandoned.

Mr. Nicholson's reasons for this were thus given by himself:—"The informant was Pat Quin; he stated he had seen five men. From conversation with Superintendent Sadleir on his return from Wangaratta it did not appear that 'the spot was indicated so that it could be found without difficulty,' nor that 'it could be taken up by the trackers at daybreak before the people were moving,' and had become conscious of the presence of the police among them. The subsequent examination by Mounted Constable Ryan as to the locality and its approaches did not tend to remove the above impression. It appeared that the neighborhood was settled, and that our party could hardly expect to pass Lloyd's house, even at midnight, without being discovered, and that the trackers might have to search over at least a quarter of a mile before finding the footprints; and, considering the precaution taken by the men seen by Quin in sending a man to dog him home, it seemed likely that they had taken the other precaution of moving off, and in different directions, so that the trackers pursuing might find themselves running down the wrong man. Sub-Inspector O'Connor was of opinion that the chance of success was a bad one. Considering my other improving sources of information, I determined on this occasion not to disturb the sense of false security into which the outlaws had been lulled. Although I decided upon the above course upon the merits of the report made to me, yet I may remind the Chief Commissioner that Quin—the informant—was the man who tried to induce me to proceed with the Benalla police and meet him at the head of the King River on the day before the Euroa Bank robbery."

So "might," and "appears," and "ifs" carried the day, and the gang again disappeared. Mr. Nicholson's system of secret spies was no more successful than any other attempts had been; and there can be no doubt it was owing to the aid given them in the district that the Kelly Gang were able to so successfully elude all their would-be captors. Jack Sherritt, a brother of Aaron, who was at this time on the look-out with the police, seems to have given valuable information, but from time to time action was deferred. There were of course always reasons for non-success forthcoming, but these reasons did not catch the Kelly gang nor avert the troubles caused by them. The second cave party organised by Mr. Nicholson was no more successful than the first, and must have been suspected by the outlaws, as well as known to the police, or they would surely have been discovered at some time or other at what had hitherto been one of their most accustomed haunts. According to accounts Mrs. Byrne's house, near which the second cave party was established, had been a favorite rendezvous of the gang, but if it continued to be so after the police were stationed near they were unable to find out.

The next heard of the gang was in connection with the theft of several mould-boards of ploughs, which were stolen from about Greta and Oxley. The thieves, however, went scot free, and though apparently vigilance was never relaxed, it was rewarded by nothing more tangible than a variety of reports and information. It is averred that the police knew the outlaws were suffering much in the way of privation, and it was strange that they were able to ascertain this and yet fail altogether to locate them. But that they did not lack necessities, and that there was not over much reliance placed on these rumors, was evidenced by the fact that the year 1880 was well advanced and the capture of the gang was apparently as far off as ever. That there was dissatisfaction over this, not only at headquarters but throughout the colony, the papers of the day bear witness, and in June Mr. Nicholson was recalled. He was allowed to prosecute the search for a month longer, but this made no difference in the state of affairs, though Mr. Nicholson left no stone unturned that might lead to capture. Success, however, was not to be his, and it must have been with feelings of no ordinary bitterness that he saw himself superseded by the officer to whom he attributed much of the coldness, strain, and suspicion that he had had to endure.

Superintendent Hare returned to the pursuit with fresh zest and energy. As he and Mr. Nicholson had always taken contrary views as to some of the best methods of carrying on pursuit, it was only to be expected that there would be many changes when the former took things in hand again. The back trackers, he fancied, kept the Kellys from another break-out, which might give the pursuers a chance to cut short their career; so that almost the first arrangement made was to send the trackers back to Queensland as soon as convenient. They had been a bone of contention between the officers engaged in the pursuit; but in spite of the ability which was fully recognised and testified by those who had had practical experience of it, these black trackers had achieved nothing in the way of terminating the Kellys' career. Aaron Sherritt, in whom Mr. Hare seems to have had most implicit confidence throughout, was soon interviewed, and found to be prolific in offers of assistance. That these came to little more than offers was due to Aaron's own career being suddenly cut short, not to the oft-prophesied treachery to the police on Aaron's part, which so many had been daily expecting.

Aaron, when he was first engaged to work with Mr. Hare, had been also engaged to marry Miss Byrne, a sister of one of the outlaws, but for some reason or other she had broken it off.

Doubtless, although Aaron and his employers seemed confident that nothing had weakened the faith the Kellys had in their former ally, some suspicion had been excited. Old Mrs. Byrne, one of the most untiring of the Kelly aids and sympathisers would have none of him, though she had not previously, as far as can be discovered, displayed any particular aversion to the proposed match. However she was evidently active in more ways than one. Aaron found himself jilted. An endeavor then to make himself acceptable to Kate Kelly came to nothing either, which seems pretty plain proof that the once popular friend of the Kellys had in some way fallen from the grace of former days in his lawless friends' eyes. However, while Mr. Hare was absent from the pursuit, Aaron found someone more amenable to persuasion than either of the sisters of the outlaws, for when Mr. Hare again took charge he found that Aaron had married and settled down.

KATE KELLY.

THE DOOM OF
AARON SHERRITT

It was the beginning of June when Mr. Hare made his fresh start after the Kellys, confident that with Aaron's help he would soon "lay them by the heels." Some of these hopes were quickly nipped in the bud, for on the evening of the 26th the death that Aaron knew would be his when the outlaws got wind of his treachery, came to him. On that evening a neighbor, Anthony Wickes, was captured by the outlaws, handcuffed, and forced to lure Sherritt from his house to his doom. Wickes was forced to call Aaron and enquire the way to his own home, and when the door was opened Joe Byrne, who had been Aaron's school-fellow and once most attached friend, fired the fatal shot. When asked afterwards why *he* did it, Joe's answer was that if he had not shot Aaron, Aaron would have shot him. Yet the murdered man had seemed ever animated by the warmest and friendli-est of feelings towards the man destined to send him to his last long account. More than once Aaron begged that Joe Byrne's life might be spared if the gang were any time encountered. This attachment does not seem to have been fully reciprocated, or it had, as in violent and uncontrolled human natures it some-times will, turned to hatred more intense than any others could be at Aaron's treachery. The second shot apparently sealed Sherritt's fate, and he apparently died without uttering a word.

Joe Byrne and Dan Kelly seem then to have taken possession of the hut in which there were four armed constables stationed there for the express purpose of capturing them. Such
abject cowardice as these men displayed is fortunately not
often exhibited by men of the British race, and even the outlaws'
conduct compares favourably with theirs. Whatever else these
last have been charged with, that of putting a woman between
themselves and danger of immediate death could not be brought
against them. This was what the constables in Sherritt's hut
did—men sworn in for the protection of their fellow-creatures.
They sought refuge under the bed, and there lay trembling for
their own miserable lives, instead of justifying their claim to the
name and nature of men. When the first shock of the news of
this murder had subsided, and the public had had time to realise
the fact that there were four fully-armed members of the police
force on the spot at the time, and that not a shot was fired in the
interests of the country, there was indignation deep and strong.
It was soon known that only two of the gang were concerned
in this outrage, for Ned Kelly and Steve Hart were at that time
making their presence felt at Glenrowan. The conduct of the constables at Sherritt's hut was *the* theme of conversation, and had
they fallen into the hands of some of the critics who felt that a
blow should have been struck in the honor of manhood if nothing
else, the treatment received would have been of anything but a
gentle character. This cowardice displayed was a stain on the
manhood of the colony, and the inquest was awaited in almost
a fever of impatience. All were anxious to hear what the constables had to say for themselves, and there were few who did not
hope that the evidence would reveal their conduct in a less reprehensible light than that which had hitherto been shed upon it.

One of the principal witnesses was Mrs. Barry, Aaron Sherritt's mother-in-law, who, with Mrs. Sherritt, knew whether the

constables in the hut made any attempt to discharge their duty. According to their account, no shots were fired by the police; but as Byrne, while talking to her outside, was careful to keep Mrs. Barry between himself and the door, this may have accounted for it. From the *Argus* report of the inquest we gather that she deposed to Constable Duross having gone into the bedroom where the other three constables were concealed directly on hearing Wickes' knock, so that none might discover the presence of the police. Aaron Sherritt seems not to have taken his neighbor's request to be shown the way home in anything but a joking spirit, and Mrs. Barry said he was pointing to a sapling "more for a lark" than to show the way. It proved the last "lark" the doomed man was to indulge in, however, for Joe Byrne immediately stepped forward and did his deadly work. Byrne then made Mrs. Barry go and see if any boards were knocked off the house, and then walked her and Anthony Wickes back home, always keeping them between himself and the door. Dan Kelly was busy in the meantime getting bushes to set fire to the house.

Mrs. Barry said—"He told me he was going to set fire to it, and asked if there was any kerosene in the house. I said, "No." He said, 'What was burning on the table?' I said, 'A candle.' I cannot say whether he set fire to the bushes or attempted to do so with matches. I only saw him going round the house picking the bushes up. Wickes was standing close to me all the time.

"Joe Byrne said—'We will burn the house.' I said, 'For God's sake don't do that, or the girl will be burnt.' He said, 'You go in and bring her out.' I said, 'If I go in I shall not be let out again perhaps. He said, 'We will see about that.' I said, 'Well, don't burn the house, whatever you do.' I then went into the house."

This witness further deposed that the police could not see Byrne through the partition, but as there was only a calico screen in the doorway between the two rooms, and the police were in darkness, which would favor the probability of those standing in the light being in some degree discernible, it is doubtful whether the plea of not being able to see carried much weight.

Byrne, when talking to Mrs. Barry, asked how many men there were in the hut, and she answered that she saw two in there. Byrne then said, "Don't say what we are about, or I will shoot you." When Aaron was shot the constables seem to have had some idea of making a fight for it, for they cocked their guns.

Byrne, however, heard them, and called out, "Hark! Look out! Do you hear, they are cocking their guns."

Mrs. Sherritt said that Byrne heard Duross going into the bedroom. He said, "Who is that man?" I said it was a man that was going to stay with us that night, that he was looking for work. Byrne said, "Bring that man out." Before that he told my mother to open the front door, and she did. Dan Kelly made his appearances then. I saw him. He had a revolver pointed at me when he came to the door.

Byrne after that called myself and my mother out to the back door. He said, "Why don't you bring that man out of the room?" I said he would not come out with me. Byrne fired two shots into the bedroom where the men were. He sent me in two or three times to get the men out. All the time he kept mother and Mr. Wickes in the front of him, shading him from the door. Byrne heard some one clicking their arms inside, and said if I did not go in and bring the man out he would shoot myself and my mother. I went inside and the men would not let me out again, as they said I would be shot. My mother was outside all this time, and Dan Kelly told her to fetch the men out or he would burn the house. I could hear him speaking to my mother. My mother afterwards came in, and two of the men shut the door.

No shots were fired by the police when I went into the bedroom after my husband was shot. The police were standing on each side of the door. If they had attempted to lift the calico screen they must have been shot down. There was a bright light in the front room, and if they had fired they must have killed my mother or Mr. Wickes, as they were in front. The police did not leave the bedroom for about two hours, then they left it to shut the door.

Aaron Sherritt

COWARDICE
OF THE POLICE

Constable Armstrong, who was in charge of the watch party in the hut, deposed that on hearing the shots he said, "Take your arms, boys, the Kellys are here!" He then heard Mrs. Barry say, "Aaron is shot." He went to the front window and knelt on the bed, intending to fire out, but could see nothing but darkness. A bullet then passed from the front quite close to his head.

The next is best told in Constable Armstrong's own words, for which I am indebted to the *Argus* report:—

"Several shots were fired, and then I heard a voice say, 'Come out and surrender, or we will roast you!' We all replied:— " 'We will die first.' I then went to the front door, and went to fire in the direction. I heard some voices, but Mrs. Sherritt and Mrs. Barry were in the way, and I could not fire. I then said, 'Boys, come, let us break portholes!' but we could not do it. I then said, 'Men, have you any suggestions to make? our conduct will be severely commented on in this matter if we do not make a bold fight.' I said, 'We will rush them; are you game to follow? I asked each man separately, and he replied, 'Yes.' We then decided to wait for a better chance, thinking they might rush us—being the attacking party—and that we might get a shot at them when the light was extinguished. We remained quiet for some time, and the candle went out. I then closed both doors. We looked out then to fire. We heard voices, but could see no one. There was talking at intervals up to about daylight.

"When it got light another constable and I went round the house, and found they had left. There was a Chinaman passing at about seven o'clock. I wrote a note and gave it to him to deliver to the police at Beechworth. I proposed going, but it was not considered advisable to separate, as another attack might be made."

The Chinaman's courage failed him, so the police had to look out for another messenger. Another Chinaman was pressed into the service, and then a miner; five messengers were sent altogether. But as no answer came, Constable Armstrong at last decided on going himself, and about one o'clock the next day the tragedy was reported at Beechworth. The evidence of one of the other constables elicited nothing that was fresh, so it was decided not to call the other two, as their evidence would be simply corroborative of what had been already given. No evidence forthcoming availed to remove the impression that the constables had displayed the basest cowardice and dastardliness, and such as was hitherto unchronicled in the history of the colony.

None knew better than the constables that while the women were in the hut they were comparatively safe, for—to quote Superintendent Hare—"the gang never behaved badly to or assaulted a woman, but always treated them with consideration and respect; although frequently compelled by the exigencies of the situation to put them to considerable inconvenience."

At the conclusion at the first part of Wickes' evidence, the foreman of the jury asked if there was any necessity to proceed further, as they were all satisfied as to the cause of Sherritt's death; but Mr. Foster decided that it was needful in the interests of justice to know all that occurred, so this avenue of escape was closed to the constables in charge, and out of their own mouths they were as fully condemned as they afterwards were by the Commission. The scene in the hut is thus described and commented on in the second Progress Report issued by that body:—

"The names of the police present were Constables Armstrong (in charge), Duross, Dowling, and Alexander. Never was there a more conspicuous instance of arrant cowardice than was exhibited by these men. Instead of attacking the outlaws or making some effort out of sheer regard for their manhood, if not for their official responsibility, they sought the protection for themselves which they should have afforded to others. Two of them—Armstrong and Dowling—lay prostrate on the floor, with their bodies partly concealed beneath a bed, under which they had thrust the wife of the murdered man, with their feet resting against her so that she could not possibly escape, in the hope that her presence would deter the outlaws from shooting them or attempting, as they had threatened, to set fire to the place. The conduct of those constables throughout the night was characterised by shameful poltroonery, which in the army would have been punished by summary expulsion from the service, with every accompanying mark of contempt and degradation."

Aaron Sherritt was only twenty-five years old when thus done to death; but though only in the flush of youth and strength, had earned such a reputation that even the suddenness of his end did not give rise to as much regret as such unlooked-for occurrences usually do. His nature was evidently villainous to a degree, and by his conduct during the last months of his life in helping to hunt down the friends who had almost put their lives in his hands, so implicitly did they trust him, he had lost the sympathy even of scoundrels. Had his offers to assist the police be prompted by any desire to in some degree retrieve the evil of his life he might have gained the respect of the better disposed members of the community, but nothing seems more plain than that he was influenced throughout by the hope of gain. So in the heyday of his youth Aaron Sherritt was sent to an unhonored grave by the man to whom he had seemingly been more attached than to any other. It was perhaps a fitting close to such a life, but that this vile deed and its intimidating effect should have been possible in a place where so many were stationed prepared to prevent it, roused the public to exasperation point when the subject of the police protection of the colony was being considered. The resignation of one of the constables who were guilty of such arrant cowardice was accepted, but the other three were dismissed from the service with all the contempt that it was possible to show. The feeling roused by Sherritt's murder will be remembered by many, and as this tragedy proved the prelude to the most sensational of all the gang had hitherto attempted it will not soon be forgotten.

From some time previous to Sherritt's death there had been rumors of some intended *coup* by the gang which was to put all they had hitherto accomplished in the shade. There was, apparently, a sort of suppressed activity throughout the district. The Kelly sympathisers seemed in some way to be all astir. Old Mrs. Byrne, who was the particular confidante of the gang, and decidedly their sturdiest and most constant friend, was more than ordinarily active, and dropped hints of some impending catastrophe that confirmed a very general belief in the nearness of the end. There was activity among the pursuing party, too, for it had been notified that the reward of £8,000 would be withdrawn after the 20th of July. As it was now well on in June, there was barely a month in which to accomplish a capture which the united resources of two colonies had been vainly taxed to effect for over a year.

Up to the time of the Jerilderie robbery Victoria played almost a lone hand in the pursuit, but after that New South Wales supplemented the reward as well as assisted in other ways. Other colonies, too, had not been idle in the matter. "Catching the Kellys" seemed to be the expedition for which numbers who had not the faintest idea of how to set about it or the difficulties they would have to encounter were anxious to volunteer. It appeared to be almost a mania for a time; and more and more marvellous does it appear that four young men were thus enabled for years to defy everything and everybody. Aaron Sherritt's murder proved the match to the fuse; it roused the people as they had never been roused before, and the police must have realised, as they apparently had not done hitherto, that they had to justify their existence as a force by capturing the bloodthirsty villains whose continued existence was a menace to all and any who conformed to the laws of the land. It was, too, a question of reward or no reward to the pursuing party. The value of time, as well as of doing something to reinstate themselves in public opinion, evidently now dawned upon them.

The air was thick with rumors. All seem to feel that the gang was near, and yet none could make even a guess as to where they would be likely to appear. That they would break out somewhere was looked upon as a certainty, and that the end was near was regarded as still more certain. There seems to have been a "do-this-time-or-die" feeling amongst all occupied in the pursuit that augured more for its speedy termination than anything else had done. That they would have well and deliberately laid plans to defeat, as well as to guard against possible atrocities, was a foregone conclusion, and one can imagine the anxiety that prevailed among the pursuing party after the first shock of the news of Aaron Sherritt's death. That this was believed to have been planned as the first act in the tragedy which the gang had boasted should "not only astonish the whole colony but the whole world," was evidenced by the after comments of the Commission appointed to enquire into the case. In their second Progress Report they concluded that:—

"The murder of Aaron Sherritt was designed as the prelude to the terrible tragedy by means of which the outlaws intended to astonish not only the Australian Colonies but the whole world. It seems manifest that they had carefully thought out and matured their plan of operations. They proposed in the first place to shoot Aaron Sherritt. By this they rightly conjectured that they would not only have wreaked their vengeance upon one who had betrayed them to the police, but would induce the authorities to despatch on the following day (Sunday), when there was no ordinary traffic on the line, a special train to Beechworth with the Queensland trackers and a large body of police. Next, it was determined to wreck this special train and shoot any constable who might escape the effects of the disaster. Finally, the coast having been thus cleared, the gang were to proceed at once to Benalla, or one of the townships in the district, rob one of the banks, and with the spoil retrace their steps to their previous haunts in the ranges. By one of those unforseen accidents which often defeat the best laid schemes, execution of the latter portion of their programme was frustrated."

THE BEGINNING
OF THE END

Aaron Sherritt finally disposed of, his murderers were free to join the leader of the gang and his aide—Steve Hart—who were busy preparing to carry out their fiendish plans at Glenrowan. This they did, riding thither from the Woolshed, the scene of their last vengeful exploit. The first step was to capture some railway line-repairers and compel them under fear of death to assist in the proposed destruction of their fellow creatures by taking up the rails. With the assistance of the gang these were taken up for about a mile, and when displaced to their satisfaction the outlaws took up their quarters in Jones's Hotel, at Glenrowan, which was soon turned into a house of detention. Prisoner after prisoner was marched into the place where the unfortunate line-repairers were awaiting the dire catastrophe which they would have helped to bring about. Glenrowan was literally captured, and any of the inhabitants who were luckless enough to approach the place where the gang were located were straightway bailed up and imprisoned. Over sixty people, including Constable Bracken, who covered himself with glory on this occasion, were secured. Though the impending disaster was known among them, and many must have listened for the approaching train with trembling hearts, but little outward sign was given. The gang, as was their custom, promoted the enjoyment of their prisoners as much as possible. Dancing and fun was the order of the evening, and in this the outlaws joined with all their hearts, while waiting for the fellow creatures they were luring on to their doom. While this was going on Superintendent Hare and the pursuing party were busy. The news of Aaron Sherritt's death startled all into instant action. The black trackers who had been despatched to Melbourne on their way home were recalled, and there was great excitement not only among the pursuers but throughout the colony. Never before had such a profound sensation been created; and it is safe to say that there were very few in the colony who did not wait further news of the Kelly gang as eagerly as those who were waiting the word of command to start after them. This start was made after some delay in connection with the trackers, and totally in the dark as to where the outlaws or some of their fiendish work might be encountered. The contingency of the rails being torn up was guarded against as much as possible by sending a pilot engine ahead, and one can imagine with what feelings its warning whistle was heard. This pilot engine had been stopped by a Mr. Curnow, the schoolmaster at Glenrowan, who, at great risk to himself and those belonging to him, had contrived to give the warning that helped to save so many lives. Mr. Curnow had, with his wife and sister, been bailed up by the Kelly gang earlier in the day, but had succeeded by a show of friendliness in gaining their confidence. He felt that he must warn those in the train of the fate prepared for them. Though delayed in many ways, and having when at liberty to resist the entreaties from those most dear to him to stay, he yet adhered to his purpose. Miss Curnow seems to have been something of the same disposition as himself, and when once her natural reluctance to see her brother go into danger was overcome, she aided him by every means in her power. Mrs. Curnow's entreaties were resisted, but while her husband was making ready, he heard the train coming. Of his conduct too much in the way of praise cannot be said. He literally took his life in his hands when he started off to stop the special, and the thought of those dearest to him being visited and perhaps shot by the bushrangers in revenge for his defection while he was away, was enough to have kept the boldest of men back from such a task. It did not keep the brave schoolmaster, however, and soon his red scarf and light were warning those on the pilot engine of the danger ahead. Mr. Curnow does not seem to have told exactly where the gang was located. He was in haste to get back to the wife and child whose lives might be the price paid for his daring, so the special was taken on cautiously to the Glenrowan station, through which it would otherwise have lashed without stopping, and carried on all to their doom had it not been for this warning. The gang knew when the train stopped that they had been thwarted in their design, and apparently also knew that the fight would now be to the death.

CONSTABLE
BRACKEN ESCAPES

The pursuing party were as yet ignorant of where in Glen-rowan the gang were to be found, and much valuable time would undoubtedly have been lost if Constable Bracken, who had been imprisoned in the hotel, had not contrived to escape. The constable had been taken into the room where the gang and their prisoners were dancing, and knowing that Dan Kelly had charge of the key watched with cool determination to get possession of it. Dan Kelly, like the rest of the gang, had evidently become somewhat over-confident of its terrorist influence, for he put the key down when dancing, and Bracken secured it. The chance to use it came when the outlaws went out to make ready for the approaching train. Their intention was to rake it with shot after it had toppled over the embankment. While they were out Bracken escaped. Had he not done so the gang would most probably have had the chance for another spell of bushranging. As it was, Bracken got to the station and gave the pursuers their first chance of getting at close quarters with the dreaded band.

It is easy to imagine the feeling of intense excitement that prevailed at Bracken's news. All the suspense and excitement of the years that had passed since the pursuit began must have been crowded into those few seconds of time. If any fear came with the tidings it must have been lost in the tumult of feelings aroused. Calling on his men to follow him, Superintendent Hare dashed off to the hotel; the horses that were being taken out of the train were left to their own devices, and the attacking party were soon at work. Although at a disadvantage, as they always had been, for the hotel was in deep shadow, while they must have been clearly distinguishable in the light of the waning moon. The odds were in favor of the outlaws in spite of their inferiority of numbers, and the moment when the three were descried upon the verandah must have been a thrilling one indeed for the men who had at last run them down. At almost the first shot Superintendent Hare was wounded, but held his ground until the outlaws were driven into the house. It was then surrounded, and all possibility of retreat cut off.

What the feelings of those inside the hotel could have been when the dreaded outlaws were forced to re-enter can only be imagined. All knew of their peculiar methods of revenge, and many must have expected that nothing less than the lives of some of the unoffending ones would have satisfied the gang when they realised that all was lost. Firing ceased for a time, during which Superintendent Hare sent messengers to other stations asking for assistance, and had his wound attended to. It proved, however, more serious than was at first anticipated, and, though the Superintendent made an effort and returned to the scene of the fight to take part in it, he had again to leave; so it went on without him. Mr. Hare left the attacking party seemingly in charge of Mr. O'Connor, the officer in charge of the trackers; but no one seemed quite sure who it devolved upon, and as Mr. O'Connor did not distinguish himself in any particular way between the departure of the one superintendent and the arrival of the other (Sadlier, from Benalla), he does not come in for over much praise for his share in the affair. The Commission Report thus comments on it:—

"Superintendent Hare, when he took his departure from the scene, appears to have been under the impression that he left Mr. O'Connor in charge of the attack. No doubt such was his intention, but Inspector O'Connor seems throughout the morning to have been animated by but one idea—namely, that by remaining in the deep cutting where he had sought shelter he was guarding the outlaws from that quarter. A little reflection, however, would have led this officer to see that if the outlaws did attempt to escape they were not likely to select the front, where they would have to run the gauntlet between the parties of police and people there stationed. If an escape were attempted at all, it was more likely to have been by the rear of the hotel, where the ground was covered with timber and scrub, while the Warby Ranges were only a short distance off. Therefore, instead of standing in the cutting blazing away every time a flash was seen from the hotel, Mr. O'Connor might just as well have been on the platform along with the ladies (for there were two from Melbourne present during the conflict), the reporters, and other non-combatants."

This was rather severe on Mr. O'Connor, but the Commission had evidently good grounds for the conclusion arrived at in regard to his conduct. Sergeant Steele arrived with reinforcements from Wangaratta, and these, with the Benalla contingent under Superintendent Sadleir, made a considerable force with which to bring the four desperadoes to terms. It was known that some among the prisoners had been wounded, but though the police endeavoured to get the women of the party to come away, it was long before any could be induced to stir. When the reinforcements appeared on the ground, however, some seemed to have made a dash of it. A Mrs. Reardon, who appeared to have almost lost her senses with terror, had a narrow escape, and her son was shot in the breast; but the fatalities were few considering the number that were packed away in the hotel. In addition to young Reardon, a child of Mrs. Jones, the proprietress of the hotel, as well as an old man (Martin Cherry) were wounded.

The excitement had now become most intense. Alive or dead the attacking party meant to have the outlaws, and it was felt that alive they would never be taken. They kept under cover, however, and all the police could do was to continue firing into where the gang were entrenched, though there was no means of knowing with what effect. The stationmaster walked boldly out of the hotel, and some women and children escaped, but the majority of the prisoners stayed voluntarily where the Kellys had put them, seemingly as much paralysed by fear of the police as they had been by fear of their captors.

Had it been known then that Ned Kelly had escaped, and that Joe Byrne was killed just before or almost simultaneously with the arrival of the Benalla and Wangaratta reinforcements, the fight might have been brought to a conclusion earlier in the day, but all were in the dark with regard to the gang, and as those in the hotel who could come out would not, the fight went on with little intermission until well on in the morning of the next day. It must have been a strange scene to have been enacted in such an age as this—the armed resources of the law set at defiance by four individuals. A great opinion of the courage of these four seemed at the time to prevail, but there was little of what could be called courage in it. It was rather a determination to have as many lives for their own as possible. These were forfeit either way. They could not get out of the colony, and death would not have been much worse, according to all accounts, that the existence they had led for some time previous to the murder of Aaron Sherritt. It was a feeling of a much baser character than courage that induced them to so hold out to the peril of unoffending fellow-creatures, that one marvels how even the unthinking could call up any admiration for what was regarded as the brute courage of the gang. Had they always fought so there might have been some claim to this quality, but hitherto they had stolen unawares on their victims and murdered with cold-blooded deliberation. So well was this known that even the criminal fraternity should have been moved to horror and disgust at their doings rather than to vainglory.

CAPTURE OF NED KELLY

The fight went on all night, the firing from the hotel seemingly slackening as day dawned. The hotel was surrounded, for though the finding of a rifle had made the besiegers by this time conclude that one of the gang had escaped, they we not certain who it might be. No thought of the chance of its being the dreaded leader occurred to these sapient members of the police force. So much had been heard from time to time throughout the career of the gang of the almost phenomenal fearlessness, strength, and courage of Ned Kelly, that had a guess been made as to the escapee it would most probably have been at any one of the gang rather than its leader. Yet, with all his reputed fearlessness, and regardless of the claim the men he had led into crime and to a violent death had upon him, he sought safety for himself in flight at an early period of the fight. It was said that "it was not the intention of the bold ruffian to desert his comrades," but it was made manifest that such was his intention if it could have been accomplished; but wounded and friendless, unable to disencumber himself of his armor, there was nothing for him but a miserable death in the bush or the more speedy and more-to-be-desired despatch by his enemies. In the newspaper report of the escape it was asserted that "he could not without danger get into the hotel, so he sprang upon his horse and during the excitement which followed

THE AUSTRALASIAN SKETCHER

Nº 101.—VOL. VIII.   MELBOURNE, SATURDAY, JULY 3, 1880.   PRICE 6d

NED KELLY AT BAY.

FROM A SKETCH DRAWN ON THE SPOT BY MR. T. CARRINGTON.

got away towards Morgan's Lookout, but that it was not the intention of the bold ruffian to desert his comrades, and he returned to fight his way to them." But there was no such sensational escape as this. The Commission Report says:—

"About seven o'clock Ned Kelly, the leader of the gang, was captured. He had been wounded in the foot during the first brush with the police. He left the hotel by the back shortly after, and selected his own horse, which he led away into the bush at the rear. On the way, and not far from the house, he seems to have dropped his rifle and the scull cap that he wore inside his iron head-piece. He then endeavored to disencumber himself of his armor, but being unable without assistance to do so he evidently made up his mind to break through the cordon of police, rejoin, and die with his companions in the hotel. His capture was effected without much difficulty or danger, as he was wounded in several parts of the body, and was incapacitated from using his revolver with effect.

As the tall figure of the outlaw, encased in iron, appeared in the indistinct light of the dawn the police for a time were disconcerted. To some it seemed like an apparition; others thought it was a black man who had donned a nail-can for a joke, but as the shots fired from Martini-Henri rifles at short range were found to have no effect, the sensation created seemed to have been akin to superstitious awe. One man described it as "the devil," another as the "bunyip." Ned Kelly advanced until within a stone's throw of the hotel, when, in the emphatic vernacular of the bush, he defied the police, and called of the members of his gang to come out of the hotel and assist him.

The *Age* says:—"The contest then became one which from its remarkable nature almost baffles description. Nine police joined in the conflict and fired point blank at Kelly; but although, in consequence of the way in which he staggered, it was apparent that many of the shots hit him, yet he always recovered himself, and, tapping his breast, laughed derisively at his opponents, as he coolly returned the fire, fighting only with a revolver. It appeared as if he was a fiend with a charmed life. For half an hour this strange contest was carried on, and then Sergeant Steele rapidly closed in, and when within about ten yards of him fired two shots into his legs, which brought the outlaw down. He was only wounded, and appeared still determined to carry on the desperate conflict, but Steele bravely rushed him and seized the hand in which he held his revolver, the only weapon with which he was armed. He fired one last shot, but without effect. When on the ground he roared with savage ferocity, cursing the police vehemently. He was then stripped of his armor and became quite submissive, and was borne to the railway station by Sergeant Steele, Constable Dwyer, and two representatives of the Melbourne Press."

Superintendent Hare said that Ned Kelly was "the only one who in any way showed the white feather," and he seems almost to have whined for mercy, evidently expecting that his captors would show him only the mercy that he had shown to the brave but ill- fated Kennedy. In the evidence given at the trial, Constable Kelly said that the outlaw—when they ran up to him as he fell—said to Bracken, who was with them, "Save me, Bracken, I once saved you." Constable Kelly answered, "You did not show poor Scanlon and Kennedy much mercy." The outlaw's reply was, "I had to shoot them or they would have shot me."

Ned Kelly captured was as different from Ned Kelly at large as those much given to braggadocio usually are. He proved more easily managed than perhaps any other member of the gang would have been, and so different was his behavior to theirs that it seems wonderful how his could have been the master spirit of the gang. All engaged in the pursuit had seemed throughout to be possessed with the idea that if they could capture the leader, or in any way separate him from the rest of the gang, its dispersion would be comparatively easy. Yet this idea was the exact opposite of what actually happened. Ned Kelly sought safety for himself in flight, and then returned only to fall an easy prey to his enemies. With the rest of the band it was victory or death. It will never be known now whether the gang agreed to Ned Kelly making his escape for, perhaps, some further purpose of revenge, or whether he basely deserted the comrades he had spurred on in their career of crime. It seems clear, however, that he would have escaped if he could, and only the impossibility of doing so, encased pretty well as he was in iron, weighing altogether 97 or 98 lbs., and from which it proved impossible to disencumber himself without assistance, brought him back to the scene of the fight. From the *Age* report of the conversation that took place after the outlaw's capture we gather that he said he could have got away if he had liked, but all who knew anything of the surroundings and condition of the man also knew that there was no chance. Much of what was said in regard to this was accepted at its true value. After saying how they were prepared to dispose of the special train and its occupants, he went on:—

"It does not much matter what brought me to Glenrowan. I do not know, or I do not say; it does not seem much anyway. If I had liked I could have got away last night. I got into the bush with my grey mare, and laid there all night. I had a good chance but I wanted to see the thing end. When the police fired the first round I got wounded in the foot—it was the left one; shortly after I was shot through the left arm. It was in the front of the house where I received these injuries. I don't care what people say about Sergeant Kennedy's death; I have made my statement as to it, and if they don't believe me I can't help that. At all events I am satisfied that Scanlon was not shot kneeling. That is not true—he never got off his horse. At the commencement of the affair this morning I fired three or four shots from the front of Jones' Hotel, but I do not know who I was firing at. I only fired when I saw flashes; I then cleared for the bush, but remained there near the hotel all night. Two constables passed close by me talking, and I could have shot them before they had time to shout if I had liked. I could have shot several constables at one time. I was a good distance away, but I came back again." Speaking of the train that was to have been wrecked, he said:—"I wanted to fire into the carriages, only the police started for us too quickly. I knew the police would come, and I expected them." You wanted, then, to kill the people in the train?" Superintendent Sadleir asked; and Kelly answered, "Yes, of course I did. God help them, they would have got shot all the same. Would they not have tried to kill me?"

The capture of the leader of the gang did not in any way expedite matters in regard to its other members. They were still in the hotel, though in what condition it was impossible to tell. It would have made things easier if the attacking party could have persuaded those imprisoned by the outlaws to come out, but this they could not be induced to do, seeming to have been almost bereft of their senses by what had occurred, and quite unable to decide on which side safety lay. When at last, and towards the middle of the day, they decided on throwing themselves on the tender mercy of the police, the scene must have been a remarkable one. Between thirty and forty men rushed distractedly out, apparently as terror stricken as women could have been, and for a time they were under the impression that they would in some way be held responsible for the doings of the day. It was several minutes before they seemed to comprehend that there was nothing but a search and examination to fear from the police. When they did, this was proceeded with, but nothing much regarding the outlaws still within the hotel was gleaned. Joe Byrne had been killed early in the day, and Dan Kelly and Steve Hart had been seen holding a consultation in the passage, but this was all that could be gathered concerning them. They were both in armor, but apparently aware that the end was near; but no one of the prisoners realised of how much importance some idea of the nature of this consultation might have been to the police. The knowledge that the outlaws were still in the house and alive did not facilitate matters much for the attacking party, for all efforts to dislodge or make them break cover proved in vain. The police continued firing into the building, but there was little attempt to return it after those who had been imprisoned at the hotel had escaped. The police were reinforced, and an excited crowd gradually increased to witness the final scenes in the Kelly's tragic career. The whole colony, in fact, was waiting in much the same state of suspense and suppressed excitement that the little crowd at Glenrowan were in. None could tell how soon the end would come, nor give even a guess at the length of time the survivors of the gang might hold out; and so impressed were they with the power and resources of the members of the gang, that they were in momentary expectation of the survivors signalising their exit by some demoniac act which would be on a par with their former achievements. All over the colony withersoever the news had flashed of Aaron Sherritt's death, news of the pursuing party again on the trail inspired afresh with hope, or shall we say premonition, of success. People were waiting almost with bated breath for the next news from Glenrowan. It was safe to say that never before had there been such a widespread and profound sensation created in the history of the colony. Those who did not know to what extremity the outlaws had been reduced, knew not what fresh and unimagined horror to look for from their hands, and those on the spot who were aware of all except the condition the survivors of the gang might be in, could not feel at all sure that some unoffending life might not yet be sacrificed in the endeavor to dislodge the outlaws.

Hostilities ceased for a while. There was suspense and uncertainty all round, and the besiegers were undecided how to act for the best. The next step taken was to telegraph to Melbourne for a field gun and ammunition to effectually dislodge the outlaws by blowing down the hotel. But events marched on without the aid of the desired gun. When the telegram had been duly sent off the fear of the gun not arriving in time to effect the purpose desired decided the besiegers on another plan for routing the outlaws. It was ultimately determined to burn them out, the horror most mortals have of this kind of death being most probably relied upon to drive forth the outlaws. Preparations for adopting this course were accordingly made. The appearance of Mrs. Skillian at this juncture caused a momentary diversion. Like all the Kellys she seemed not adverse to creating a sensation, and in a riding habit faced with scarlet and a showy feather, little in keeping with the dreadful fate that awaited one of the brothers, to whom she had apparently been so devoted. She was earnestly besought to use her influence with the outlaws to induce them to surrender, but she said sooner than do this she would prefer to see her brother burned in the house. So the proposed plan was put into operation. One member of the police made his way to the house with a bundle of straw, while the others opened fire on the front and rear of the hotel to divert attention from his proceedings. It must have been a terrible moment for those watching the scene, for it was known that an old man who had been wounded at the beginning of the fray had been left in the building with the outlaws. Kate Kelly, too, had by this time joined the crowd, and the thought of the two sisters of one of the men in the house must have added considerably to the feeling of horror that fell upon them.

Much sympathy was expressed for any sisters obliged to look on at the preparations for such a dreadful death for their brother, and this was added to by Mrs. Skillian rushing forward and exclaiming, "I will see my brother before he dies!" But she did not go far; the orders of the police cooled her ardor, and she fell back among the crowd. There is no doubt that she and Kate Kelly excited a good deal of sympathy for themselves, and perhaps some hard feelings against the besiegers and their plan. At the same time the Kelly family were given to do so much for effect, and sympathy-rousing had been such a stock-in-trade of the whole family, as well as the gang, that it is doubtful whether they felt as much as seemed apparent to the crowd. Their after conduct did not seem to convey the idea of very deep grief for their brothers being possible. They were, however, the object of very general commiseration on the occasion of the outlaws' cremation, and one marvels how any possessed of woman's heart or nature could stand by while preparations for so terrible an end were being made.

The horror that possessed the crowd was, however, more for the wounded platelayer who was in the hotel with the outlaws than for the recreants themselves. All felt sure that the flames would drive these two out, but it was known that Cherry was helpless, and must thereby perish, if no one went to his assistance. Some one did, however; a Roman Catholic priest—Father Gibney—who was among the crowd volunteered to save him. As this father went in the hotel door the flames burst out, and the horror-stricken crowd seemed to feel that they had looked their last on the brave clergyman. Animated by the desire to save him, some policemen burst in at the back, and were, with Father Gibney, successful in bringing out the body of Byrne, as well as the wounded man. Dan Kelly and Hart were, it was reported, lying dead upon the floor, but nothing could be attempted in regard to them until the fire had completed its work. With the raking out of the charred skeletons this dreadful scene came to an end, and to the many friends, relations, and sympathisers of the gang among the assembled crowd it should have proved how tragically a career of crime rewards those who deliberately pursue its downward course.

Of the four who by such fearful means had achieved their desire for notoriety and fed their passion for revenge, there was only one left to suffer the death which the whole gang had determined should never be theirs—this one, the leader, who might have been expected to die at his post rather than make any move which would expose him to the risk of being captured. Instead of which, however, he seems to have deliberately deserted his comrades in crime at the moment when he who had led them into it should have stood most staunchly by. Had the escape been pre-arranged Ned Kelly would undoubtedly have made the fact known, for even up to the last he was busy in the work of self-justification. It seems as if this act should for ever have dispelled the idea of his having been in any way as brave as he was represented to be by himself and others. It looks, rather, as if he was the least courageous of the gang, and as if even the criminal classes must fail to see anything heroic in his life of deeds.

Those who investigated the circumstances of the last scene in the lives of the other outlaws were satisfied that Dan Kelly and Steve Hart had committed suicide before the building was fired, which in part removed the feeling of horror which the plan had inspired. There had been no reply to the firing of the police for some time before this ceased, and it was thought that the outlaws were keeping quiet until nightfall, when they would most probably try to make good their escape. With the cordon formed by the police round the house, however, and the fact of the horses left ready saddled and bridled at the back having been shot, there was not much chance of this. So it seems almost certain that the two desperadoes must have elected to die by their own hands rather than by those of their would be captors. There was no means of ascertaining this, however, for though Superintendent

Sadlier was repeatedly urged to consent to a rush being made on the hotel he would not consent, having determined that not another life should be sacrificed in the capture of the outlaws.

The Commission comment at this juncture observes:—"The Superintendent was very probably influenced by humane motives in arriving at this decision, but a dispassionate observer could not fail to couple this inactivity with a want of capacity, if not of courage, to deal with the difficulty. Of course, if an attack were made as suggested, the officer in charge was in honor bound to take the lead, so that if there were danger in having recourse to such an expedient the spectators could not be blamed if they thought more of Mr. Sadleir's discretion than of any other quality displayed on that very trying occasion. The spectators were clearly not that day impressed with a very elevated opinion of police proceedings."

NED KELLY SENT
TO MELBOURNE GAOL

Ned Kelly was sent on to Melbourne, where he received the medical attention necessary to make him in a fit condition to stand his trial for the Wombat murders. His arrival there created an immense sensation. The remains of the other outlaws were given to their relatives, and over the charred skeletons of Dan Kelly and Steve Hart a great wake was held! Ned Kelly had still to stand his trial, but his fate was a foregone conclusion, so that the gang who for years had been the terror of the colony was at last effectually disbanded, though while one of them remained alive the sensational interest would not die.

With the destruction of the gang came of course congratulations from all over the colony. Those who had taken part in and accomplished it were regarded as heroes, and it was not until the publication of the results of dispassionate investigation by the Commission of Enquiry that people were enabled to form clear ideas of the prowess that was respectively displayed. The Governor of Victoria, as well as the Chief Secretary, telegraphed to Superintendent Hare congratulating on the bravery displayed by himself and men; but whatever the Commission thought of the wisdom or otherwise of general conduct, their reflections on Mr. Hare's conduct were rather scathing. After disposing of the idea that any extraordinary foresight was displayed in providing a pilot engine, when the report current of the rails having been taken up had made this precaution necessary, and censuring Mr. Hare for tolerating the presence of ladies in the special when he knew the dangers they would be exposed to, the Commission Report proceeds:—

"We consider this officer cannot be complimented upon his discretion or generalship in the conduct of operations at Glenrowan for the short time that he remained upon the scene. He knew apparently little of the precise situation of Glenrowan, notwithstanding that he had been for eight months in command of the district. He was informed during the journey that the Kellys had torn up the rails, taken possession of the place, and imprisoned all the people there, yet on arrival he apparently had no correct idea of the peculiarity of the situation. The moment he was informed by Bracken of the presence of the outlaws at the hotel he dashed away without waiting for some of his men to collect their arms. When he reached the hotel he found his onslaught resisted by the gang. He was disabled in the wrist by the first volley, and after an absence of from five to ten minutes from the platform returned to have his wound dressed. He left the front without transferring the command to any one. The order to surround the hotel given to Senior Constable Kelly and to Inspector O'Connor cannot be regarded as transferring the command. This neglect he might have rectified when he essayed to reach the front on the second occasion, but he failed to do so. Did he propose to rush the place and at once overpower the outlaws? If that were his intention he should not have been deterred by a mere wound in his wrist from doing so. If he had resolved merely to surround the gang and prevent their escape then he ran unnecessary risk in exposing himself and his men to the fire of the outlaws. If, however, he simply trusted to a chapter of accidents, without any definite idea of what was best to be done, then his management of affairs displayed a decided lack of judgement and forethought. Comparisons may be odious, but it cannot fail to strike one as singular that while Superintendent Hare felt himself obliged to leave his post and return to Benalla under the impression that the wound in his wrist would prove fatal, the leader of the outlaws—with a rifle bullet in his foot and otherwise wounded in the extremities—was enabled to hold his ground encumbered, too, by iron armour until seven o'clock, when in his efforts to rejoin his companions he fell overpowered by numbers."

Mr. Hare, in explaining his motives for allowing ladies to accompany a party sent on so dangerous an errand, says that he allowed them to accompany the party intending that they should remain at Beechworth while the officer in charge of the trackers, to whom one of the ladies in question had been recently married, followed in the tracks of the outlaws. But it is difficult to see how Mr. Hare could have thought this, if, as he stated previously, he really was convinced that the special train never would reach Beech-worth, one feels dubious as to how to reconcile such conflicting statements, and many readers will probably have concluded ere this that Mr. Hare was not singularly regardless of the safety of the ladies, he must have been anything but as convinced of the immediate danger of the situation as he claimed to have been.

The *Age* report of these ladies' conduct is:—"They retained their seats in the railway carriage, and the courage they displayed, notwithstanding that the bullets from the outlaws whistled past them, surely ought to have a good effect on the men who were facing death in the execution of duty." The Commission, however, took an exactly opposite view. Their verdict was, "That it was a mistake to have allowed ladies to accompany the party from Melbourne, and, as a fact, their presence had the reverse of an inspiriting influence upon the officer in charge of the Queensland contingent who was practically in command of the attacking party during the interval between the departure of Superintendent Hare and the arrival of Superintendent Sadlier." So to mistakes all round the tardiness with which matters in connection with the Kelly gang were brought to a conclusion was evidently due.

The Kelly gang were disposed of, it was true. Three of them had been sent to their last account, while the leader was helpless and under medical care; but the trouble was not over. It certainly seems a ghastly idea that of curing a man only to subsequently kill him. But bad as he was, and many as were the rights to consideration to citizenship he had forfeited, Ned Kelly had as much claim to be put into fit condition for arraignment as the best man on earth. Every care was given to him, and he was sent from Benalla on to the Melbourne Gaol, at which he was the chief attraction during his stay. From here—as enquiry elicited the fact that he had no objection to the trial taking place there—he was remanded to Beechworth. He was fairly respectful in demeanour on some occasions, but on the morning of his removal he was insolent in the extreme. He was removed so quietly that few knew the noted outlaw, who would return only to his death, was being removed, so there was none of the sensation and crowds there would have been if any hint of his intended departure had been given. He was cautioned that he had better behave quietly, and his reply was, "I am quiet, ain't I?" but the advice made little difference in his manner. At Newmarket, where it was necessary to cross the line when changing, he refused to walk over, saying that the Government was rich enough to pay for a conveyance for him, and from this he would not budge. Argument and remonstrance were of no avail. In fact, he seems to have behaved as if utterly careless of consequences, or as a man who was so certain of acquittal that he was under no necessity to propitiate his captors. It is not easy to see how any such certainty could be felt, unless he thought the Kelly influence and the adoration of the criminal classes might yet be sufficient to save him from the death he dreaded. It is more probable, however, that he knew there was nothing to be either lost or won, and behaved with the recklessness such knowledge inspires in men of his stamp. There was a strong body of police in the carriage with him, and Ned Kelly beguiled the time in characteristic fashion. The arrival at Beechworth was unmarked by any demonstration, and the last of the Kelly Gang was soon in close captivity, and awaiting the trial to which hundreds were looking forward with an interest which never before or since in Victoria has been equalled for intensity.

Of all that had happened during the lawless career of the gang Ned Kelly was the only one who could speak positively, and though it was hardly probable that he would choose to give the whole truth and nothing but the truth, yet there was a possibility of learning a great deal more than could be learned from any one else.

The trial commenced on the 6th of August, and throughout the colonies feverish impatience to read every word and grasp every point seemed the feeling most generally manifested. Among the crowd gathered at the trial were numbers of the Kelly sympathisers as well as friends. There were bonds of relationship as well as of pursuits between so many present, that some must have thought it little wonder the gang eluded their captors for so long. There was another reason for it, too. Though for some time before the Glenrowan affair it was known that they had to suffer great privations, and that their funds were pretty well exhausted, yet it was also known that the outlaws had ever been freehanded. The pecuniary benefits of their evil deeds were freely shared with those who helped or sympathised with them, and this liberality aided greatly in the success of endeavours to keep their enemies at bay.

Superintendent Hare says:—"The gang was lavish with its money. They subsidised largely—instituting a body of spies known as 'bush telegraphs,' who kept them fully informed of every movement of the authorities, and aided them to elude capture on all possible occasions." This subsidising must, however, of necessity have been greatly curtailed, for in the Commission Report we read:—"About the months of May and April the police ascertained that the outlaws were reduced to great straits. Over a year had elapsed since their last—the Jerilderie—raid. Their funds were well nigh exhausted. With their money running short their friends and sympathisers began to fall off, and more than one, it was stated, had significantly suggested that another bank should now be robbed."

This suggestion, however, was not destined to be carried out. The bravery of Mr. Curnow, the school teacher, prevented the catastrophe which was to be the prelude to another bank robbery, and the Kelly gang were afterwards rendered harmless for further mischief. That the ill-gotten gains they were enabled to distribute was not the only bond between the gang and those who had assisted them was evidenced by not only the great number of sympathisers who watched every turn of the trial, but by the warmth of feeling displayed for the outlaw, as well as the endeavours made to save him from the death which is the price that has inevitably to be paid at last for such evil work as that of the Kellys.

The witness whose evidence was awaited with the greatest anxiety was Constable McIntyre—the one constable who escaped being murdered at the Wombat tragedy. Among the great crowd assembled, not half of which could be accommodated in the building, there was an almost hostile feeling against McIntyre. There was an impression abroad that he had abandoned the ill-fated Sergeant Kennedy when he should have stayed at his side. It says something, therefore, for the manner in which Constable McIntyre's evidence was given that it created something very like a reaction in his favor. Then it was beginning to be realised that had McIntyre not escaped the fate of the others would never have been known, and some of those who had been loudest in their denunciation of his cowardice were fain to regard his conduct in a less condemnatory light, and to think that presence of mind would more fitly describe it.

There was little more given in the evidence by this witness than the reader is already acquainted with, and nothing that was fresh could be revealed about the manner of Sergeant Kennedy's death. To the bravery of the Sergeant, Ned Kelly bore ungrudging witness. He said he was the bravest man he had ever met, and even went to the trouble of getting a cloak from the camp to cover the body, as a mark of the respect he felt for the spirit that had animated it. In respect to the exact manner of Sergeant Kennedy's death, however, even Ned Kelly kept silence. That it was cold-blooded to a degree was made evident by all that was said about it; but had the account given in the *Australasian* of June 5th been proved beyond doubt, Ned Kelly would have stood more chance of being lynched than of coming legally to his end. This account said:—"Sergeant Kennedy's life was taken in a very cold-blooded manner. He was only wounded on the day of the encounter, and was allowed to live all night so that the gang might learn from him how to work the Spencer rifle. On the following morning Ned Kelly shot him through the breast." What the outlaw himself said was:—"Kennedy and I were firing at one another. Kennedy retreated from tree to tree; one of his shots went through my whiskers and another through the sleeve of my coat, so he must have been a good shot. I followed him and he turned, I thought to fire again; he raised his arms as if to aim, when I again fired, hitting him under the armpit. He then fell. Kelly said, too, that the gang wanted to leave the ground, and did not like to leave Kennedy in a dying state, so shot him to end his misery; and that he said to Kennedy—"I will have to go, and as I do not want to leave you in a dying state, I will have to shoot you."

Kennedy's prayer to be allowed to live to bid his loved ones good-bye was unheeded, and Ned Kelly then shot him and covered him with a cloak. This was all that could be ascertained about the death that exercised the public mind the most. The details of subsequent outrages were published almost as fully after they were committed as they were given at the trial, so though every word was followed with closest attention, very little that was fresh was learned.

Next in interest to the Wombat murders came the Glenrowan affair, then fresh in the public mind. Other events faded in interest before these two, for all others had been prosaic matters of robbery and detail—no unprovoked fiendishness as in the case of poor Kennedy, and no sensationalism such as fixed the Glenrowan tragedy in men's minds. Of the varying accounts of this, none are clearer than that given by Mr. Curnow, the schoolmaster, whose heroic endeavours prevented the catastrophe on which the outlaws had relied to astonish the world and to glut their own passion for revenge. His evidence was to the effect that he was taking his family out for a drive, and on nearing Mrs. Jones's Hotel was surprised to see a number of people gathered about it. His first thought was that Mrs. Jones, who had been ill, was dead, but he was soon undeceived by the stationmaster at Glenrowan. This gentleman informed Mr. Curnow that the Kellys were there, but not dreaming that he was in earnest Mr. Curnow made as if to drive over the crossing. The truth of Mr. Stanistreet's statement was then made apparent to him. One of the gang, who he afterwards discovered to be Ned Kelly, stopped him at once, and after hearing who they were and whither they were going, ordered them to get down out of the buggy, which they did. Mr. Curnow, after he had secured the horse and buggy, was not long in discovering the intentions of the gang. He was horrified at the thought of the lives that were to be sacrificed, and seemed to have made up his mind at once that it should not occur if he could prevent it. He set about this very cleverly, and by dint of courage and address won the gang over to regard him as a staunch friend and sympathiser. He tried in various ways to induce Ned Kelly to go out with him in the hope that the constable of the place would recognise the outlaw and thereby become acquainted with what was going forward; but the Kellys discovered that they would have to pass the police barracks, and so decided not to venture.

So Mr. Curnow had to join the prisoners in the hotel, while his mind was filled with the determination to prevent the fiendish outrage contemplated by the gang. If he could only get permission to take his wife and family home he felt that he could devise something to baffle the gang in their design. This permission was very difficult to get, however, and the heroic schoolmaster must have almost despaired of being able to accomplish anything. The thought flashed into his mind that the red scarf his sister was wearing would make a splendid danger signal. He, after a little conversation with the stationmaster, gained the good graces of the gang by informing them that Mr. Stanistreet was in possession of a loaded revolver, which information won the outlaws completely. Mr. Curnow seemed to enter into their plans with all his heart. After a long delay he succeeded in getting permission to take his family home. He then had to wait for two or three hours before Ned Kelly, who insisted on accompanying them, was ready. The outlaws were in their armor, though no one suspected the cause of their tremendous bulk. On their way the Glenrowan constable was captured, and when Ned Kelly and all he had brought with him were ready to turn back to Jones' Hotel with their new prisoner, Mr. Curnow and his family were at last allowed to go home. Mr. Curnow's hindrances were not all disposed of, however. His wife and sister endeavored to dissuade him from the attempt to save the special. Fears for his and their own personal safety made them persevere, but fortunately without avail. Mr. Curnow was not to be moved from his purpose, and, seeing this, his sister at last gave way, and helped him in every way she could—principally in soothing Mrs. Curnow.

Free, at last, he was preparing to start when he heard the train coming in the distance. He ran then with the red scarf—candle and matches ready. Under Providence he was able to stop the train, and thus prevented what was intended to be a massacre as well as a railway disaster. The signal caught the eye of the guard on the engine that preceded the special. He stopped, jumped down, and was soon made acquainted with the peril they had escaped. The pilot engine went back, and Mr. Curnow, who, now he had discharged what he considered was only his duty, hastened home, as he could not rest while his own family were in peril. He attempted later on to find out how things were going at Glenrowan Hotel, but was sent back by the police. On getting home again he found that the family had been frightened almost out of their wits by a visit from a Mr. Rawlings, who afterwards distinguished himself for bravery in the affray with the bushrangers. Little knowing how these last were occupied, they thought it was one of the gang come to pay their promised visit of inspection, and felt, too, most probably, that their last hour had come.

The reader who has been privileged to wander in imagination to where Mr. Curnow could not penetrate—the scene of the fight—knows as he could not have known how things had progressed. Numbers of those present at Ned Kelly's trial were, through the medium of the Press, so fully acquainted with every detail of the tragic affair that it is almost wonderful to think of the keenness of the interest that was maintained to the end. The least interested, apparently, was the prisoner himself; but the reader will most probably feel impressed, as all others were, at the fact that even to the last Ned Kelly hoped for a reprieve from death, even though he could not hope to escape punishment of some sort; that, too,

ADELAIDE EDITION. SATURDAY,

DESTRUCTION OF THE KELLY GANG: STOPPING THE SPECIAL TRAIN BY MR. CURNOW.

he placed great confidence in the efforts for mitigation that he knew would be made by his numberless friends and relations.

There was much interest evinced in the evidence that would be given by Senior-Constable Kelly, who, it will be remembered, was ordered to surround the house when Mr. Hare's wound obliged him to leave the scene of attack, and who would thus have been held mainly responsible for the success of any attempt made by the outlaws at escape. From the *Argus* report, Kelly seems to have given a very lucid account of the circumstances of Ned Kelly's capture.

"I was present," the constable stated, "at the capture of the prisoner at Glenrowan. He appeared in the bush about seven o'clock. He looked a strange sight. He wore an oilskin coat and some sort of head-gear. Some of the police challenged him, and ordered him to go back. He took no notice of them so they fired at him, and he fired back with a revolver either at Constable Phillips or Constable Arthur, who were nearest him. I came round from the east corner of the hotel. Several other constables stood forward and fired at him. The prisoner fired at them several times, and then went behind a tree. We fired more shots at him there, but they had no effect upon him except when they struck his hand, which was round the tree. He then walked to a dead log about ten yards distant. Sergeant Steele then came from the hotel side and got within fifteen or twenty yards and fired two shots in succession. I was about twenty yards from the prisoner, and I saw him stagger under Steele's shot. I said to Constable Bracken and others, 'Come on, we will rush him.'

"With that Sergeant Steele rushed forward, fired, and Kelly again staggered. Steele fired again, when Kelly fell, saying, "That will do, Steele.' Steele seized him first and I second. We disarmed him, and found him clad in armour. We took it off, when Sergeant Steele at once recognised him as Ned Kelly. When the men run up he said to Bracken, 'Save me, I saved you.' I said,

'You showed very little mercy to poor Kennedy and Scanlon,' and he replied, 'I had to shoot them, or they would have shot me.' "I searched him on the spot, and asked, "Have you Sergeant Kennedy's watch, or will you tell me where it is, as I promised Mrs. Kennedy I would get it for her?' He replied, 'I cannot tell you; I would not like to tell you.' "The armor was made of steel mould-boards, I believe. The helmet was open at the top, with a slit for the eyes. The breast and back plates came down to his thighs, and there was a flap hanging in front. Some of the pieces were marked with the name of Hugh Lemmon, the plough maker. The prisoner when fighting with the police struck his helmet several times with his revolver, when it rang like a bell." The remainder of Constable Kelly's evidence was little more than a repetition of events with which the public had been made familiar.

TRIAL AND EXECUTION

Ned Kelly was tried at the Central Criminal Court, Melbourne, in October, and the trial, while it lasted, was certainly the sensation of the day, and monopolised much public attention, though nothing more was revealed by it than was already known. It proved a useful object lesson, for, until the Kelly sympathisers turned up as they did in force at this trial, the firm believers in the far-reaching effects of nineteenth century civilization and Christianity never realised what an uncivilised and uncontrolled humanity might live almost at their very doors. A most unsavory crowd those same sympathisers apparently were. The prisoner and his immediate relatives, Kate Kelly and Mrs. Skillian, were regarded with something very like adoration. After an exhaustive trial, which occupied two days, the prisoner was found guilty. No other verdict could have been expected, though he professed to have looked for something different. It was half expected that there would be trouble with the immense crowd assembled, but the services of the large number of police who were present ready to prevent it were not required.

The condemned man had not much to say in his own defence; perhaps he knew it was useless, or possibly he relied on the efforts of his friends and relatives to get a reprieve. As was his custom, he made still another endeavor to awaken the public sympathy. According to his own account he had been driven into a career of crime by the ill-treatment of the police; but the whole history, as well as the verdict of the Board of Enquiry went to disprove this. Ned Kelly said people who lived in large towns had no idea of the tyrannical conduct of the police in country places far removed from the courts of justice, or of the harsh, over-bearing manner in which they executed their duty, neglecting their work and abusing their powers. But the Commission of Enquiry held, "That after careful examination your Commissioners have arrived at the conclusion that the police in their dealings with the Kellys and their relations were simply desirous of discharging their duty conscientiously, and that no evidence had been adduced to support the allegation that either the outlaws or their friends were subjected to persecution at the hands of the police." So Ned Kelly's endeavours to justify himself were fruitless. If, as he said, he was "the last to curry favor or to dread the public frown," his conduct in taking every opportunity to exhibit his own actions in the best light possible to audience he held captive, not by eloquence, but by revolver and key, was strangely at variance with his words. These he knew would be caught at by enterprising reporters and published as soon after the release of those audiences as possible. So if he did not dread the public frown, he most assuredly tried to curry favor not once but many times during his career of crime.

The outlaw was sentenced to be hanged, and was taken back to gaol to await his doom. "While there is life there is hope," even in the breast of the vilest, and until the date fixed for the execution friends and relatives were unremitting in their efforts to obtain a reprieve. The answer of the Chief Secretary to the deputation which waited upon him was that Ned Kelly's case would be further considered at a special meeting of the Executive, but he could hold out no hope. At this meeting it was decided to let the law take its course. Mr. Hamilton, Mrs. Skillian, and two of the Lloyds, who tried to obtain an interview with the Executive Council while the meeting was being held, were unsuccessful, and their decision, it was hoped, would put an end to the agitation. It did not, however, and a mass meeting was held, at which there were upwards of four thousand people present.

A committee was appointed to wait on the Governor and endeavor to get him to exercise his prerogative of mercy, but His Excellency refused to receive them, and Parliament House was next invaded, but with no more success. A reprieve for a week was asked, so that petitions from various parts of the country might be presented, but Mr. Berry at once assured them of the hopelessness of their endeavor, and further said: "That the continuation of such an agitation was the unkindest and cruellest thing those who encouraged it could be guilty of; they should let it cease, and allow the doomed man to prepare to meet his fate, which was now inevitable." Later on he said: "The agitation was useless, as no power on earth could successfully intervene between the condemned man and his richly deserved doom." Even with this the agitation did not cease. Kate and James Kelly, Mrs. Skillian, Wild Wright, with others of the class, fortified by the presence of Messrs. W. Gaunson and T. Caulfield, who were obnoxiously prominent throughout what was termed the "Gaunson-Kelly demonstration," attempted to hold another mass meeting, but the police, who were there in force, stopped it, and Ned Kelly suffered the extreme penalty of the law.

His mother's last words to him were—"Mind you die like a Kelly," but his oft-vaunted courage failed him at the last. He was completely unnerved, and the priest who was in attendance had as much as he could do to keep him up at all. With his death the career of the gang, which had been the terror of the North eastern district, finally closed. But troubles many and long-continued came on those who had been concerned in the pursuit. On the country, too, for the totting up of the sums that had been expended over the capturing of the gang revealed a total that must have taken away the breath of many worthy people who fancied they knew something of the cost incurred.

Then, too, the scandal and disgrace of that deputation and procession to Government House—headed by Messrs. W. Gaunson, Hamilton, Caulfield, and four others as a committee—could not soon be forgotten. It was such a revelation, that of the "Gaunson-Kelly" demonstration. Few could have dreamed of such a manifestation of sympathy for such a man—if "man" Ned Kelly could be called.

The Geelong *Times*, in referring to the demonstration, says:— "Such an event reads like a page from the Newgate calendar. Indeed, it is a pity, seeing that it was the 5th of November, that Mr. Gaunson could not have borrowed the condemned criminal for that occasion and exhibited him to the multitude for their sympathy. Jack Sheppard's gaolers did this, charging one shilling to the general public and a crown to the nobility, and realised £200 by the venture! Dr. Dodds, the forger, made money for his exhibitors after the same fashion. Gaunson, the younger, and Kate Kelly were in the present case substituted for the greater attraction, and the morbid curiosity of the rabble had to be satisfied with the lesser sensation and the consolation that the show was free. But the whole affair is too nauseous to jest about. It is a grave outrage on society. Not the application for the reprieve, but the manner of it, and it will not be forgotten that the man who has done this thing is Mr. David Gaunson, a member of the bar, and Chairman of Committees in Parliament!"

The Ballarat *Star* said:—"It is just as well no question was asked in Parliament respecting the disgraceful part played by one of its members during the closing scene of the Kelly business, while the last dread sentence of the law remained unexecuted. Now, however, that this interesting pet of the Gaunson Brothers, this cold-blooded murderer and train wrecker, on whose behalf the maudlin sympathies of the dregs of society were enlisted, has gone to his account, it behoves the Assembly to vindicate its honor which has been besmirched by the behavior of one of its principal officers. The retention of Mr. David Gaunson in his position as Chairman of Committees is an insult alike to the electors and the Assembly."

Throughout the colony the indignation of the people found vent. The Press, too, left no word unpublished that would express the feeling of the country at such a disgusting and disgraceful demonstration. Yet this was not the only one in connection with the business, for Kate Kelly, who has been conspicuous throughout the history, made herself more so after her brother was executed. She showed herself a thorough larrikiness, and though apparently much devoted to her brothers and their interests, was also consumed with a like desire for notoriety. The opportunity to gratify this, and make money besides, was a temptation which even her sisterly affection was powerless to resist, and she allowed herself to be publicly exhibited the night after Ned Kelly's execution. Here is one of the newspaper comments on this disgusting exhibition of callousness:—

"A visit to the Apollo Hall revealed the fact that there are people insensible to all the decencies and decorum of life. On the platform of the hall were seated side by side Kate Kelly and her brother James, the female holding a bunch of flowers. Here they sat and composedly met the gaze of the Bourke Street larrikins. A more inhuman and disgraceful exhibition under the circumstances cannot well be imagined. It only lacked one thing— Messrs Gaunson, Caulfield, and Hamilton to distribute the bills."

This was such an outrage on all sense of decency that the Government interfered. The exhibition was stopped; but this was more than Kate Kelly was, for she went off to Sydney, but the Government of that colony were no more prepared to endure her presence in public than were the authorities of Victoria, so that Kate

Kelly's enterprise in the exhibition line received a sudden and final check. It was not permitted, and the curtain at last fell upon the Kelly tragedy, which had had such far-reaching and varied effects.

KELLY IN THE DOCK.—A SKETCH FROM LIFE

AUSTRALASIAN SKETCHER

No. ... VOL. VIII.   ADELAIDE EDITION. SATURDAY, NOV. ..., ...   PRICE 6d.

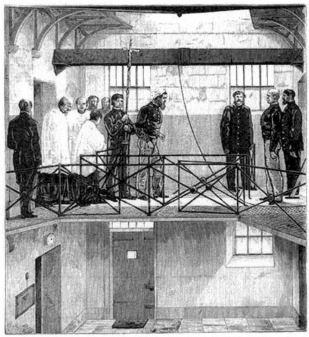

LAST SCENE OF THE KELLY DRAMA—THE CEREMONY ON THE SCAFFOLD

NOTES AND COMMENTS

That out of all the evil worked by them some little good has come is evidenced by the fact that though much in the way of threat and denunciation was indulged in, and the revengeful feeling against the police force characterising the criminal classes was intensified for a while by the fate that befell the Kelly gang, there was no attempt to form another such bushranging party. It was all very well while there was only the abstract idea of the perils and privations of such a career. The freedom of the bush, and freedom, too, from the many trammelling influences of civilization, with the daring and dash the gang had exhibited on more than one occasion, had captivated the the thoughts of many of the lawlessly-inclined; but after the gang had finally paid the dread penalty of their misdeeds in sudden and awful deaths, some better knowledge and ideas of the price they had had to pay in life began to be realised. The glamour of romance was slowly dispelled, and though the wish to set all laws at defiance, and the glory in shocking the law-abiding community was too inbred to be quickly cast off, few were prepared to follow in the footsteps of the Kelly gang, and none attempted it. Trouble was expected from many quarters, but criminality had received a salutary lesson. Though, as a rule, little disposed to profit by lessons of any description, yet that taught by the destruction of the Kelly gang was too convincing to tempt any continuation of such work.

This was one way in which some little good was derived from the years made memorable by the Kellys' doings. Another was the examination into and reorganization of the police force, which was from thenceforward able to meet its back-block foes on a more equal footing. Some little good, but what a price was paid for it in money, in lives, and in suffering? besides the criminality the Kelly outbreak seemed to let loose upon the law-abiding of the community in the large area the Kellys and their associates elected to consider their own for cattle raiding and other nefarious practices. From the Commission Report the reader may gather some idea of the extent of this:—"The Kelly country may be said to embrace the triangular track lying between the points formed by townships of Mansfield, Benalla, and Beechworth, together with the country lying to the west of the line of railway which extends to the Murray, including the vicinity of Lake Rowan, the Warby Ranges, and the neighborhood of the Woolshed. This constitutes a large and diversified extent of territory measuring about 16,000 miles." And within this 16,000 miles criminality was rampant ere the Kelly gang set the example of open defiance to the law.

The trouble that ensued was, as the reader now knows, great and long-continued. From April, 1878, the attack upon Constable Fitzpatrick was made, till June, 1880, when the destruction of the Kelly gang was at last accomplished, the Kellys were in hiding; and after the Wombat murders, in which Byrne and Hart first appear as members of the gang, the keeping down of criminal tendencies in the Kelly country could have been no easy task.

Under any circumstances it must have been most arduous, and its difficulties were doubled and trebled by the disorganization among the police force stationed throughout the district. When there is strain and dissention between officers, inefficiency, which is a natural consequence of favoritism among those under them, is bound to follow. So crime throve, for conditions were in every way favorable. In addition to all this, the cost had far outrun any estimate that had been first formed. In fact, the whole Kelly episode reads like a romance of the olden time, and even now it is difficult to realise how completely the pursuing party were at times driven to their wits end. The lack of resource in many of those engaged in the pursuit was made plain more than once, and never more so than in the Glenrowan climax.

Commenting on this some four years ago, Superintendent Hare says:—"It seems hardly possible to imagine that ten years ago a field-gun was being dragged up Collins Street, Melbourne, to blow down a hotel, which practically was little more than a wooden hut and within two hundred yards of one of the principal stations of the main line of railway between Melbourne and Sydney, as the last resource for the capture of four men who for the previous two years had set law, order, the Government, and the police at absolute defiance." Nor is it much more easy of credence that the destruction of this gang should have cost the State, from first, to last, over £115,000; and yet these are facts that cannot be controverted.

But if Mr. Hare was scathing in his criticism of Superintendent Sadlier's action *in re* the field-gun incident, the Commission was no less severe upon the "discretion or generalship in the conduct of operations at Glenrowan displayed by Mr. Hare." In fact it seems as if those who were from time to time in charge of the pursuit should have been the last to criticise each other's actions, for the Commission Report made nothing more apparent than the fact that there was blame of one sort or another to be attached to all concerned. Mr. Nicholson, who, from the way he was persecuted, and from the charges afterwards proved to be unfounded, brought against him, was in every way retarded in the discharge of his duty, and really seems the least blameworthy of all. When the long delay in the capture of the gang, and the cost incurred through it, were thus in a great measure due to the personal feuds and jealousies which almost mastered some of the officers to whom the capture was entrusted, it appears as if the methods employed should be exempt from criticism on the part of those in the pursuit invested with a little brief authority.

The long delay was over at last. Ned Kelly, the only member of the gang who survived the Glenrowan tragedy, had been sent to his last account, and his relatives and friends had been made to see that all attempts to pander to the morbid curiosity of the criminal classes, and rouse their maudlin sympathies, would be put down with an iron hand. So they dispersed, and by degrees the community began to return to something like its normal condition. Only something, however, for even those in society, who seldom concern themselves with the affairs of any not in their own particular circle, were roused out of their indifference to all that did not effect their own places and positions. The procession to Government House was a terrible revelation, and the crowds, composed of the very dregs of society, that turned out at every opportunity to demonstrate their sympathy with the last surviving member of the Kelly gang, shocked even the most indifferent. That procession and those crowds were a scandal and disgrace to the community; of that there can be no manner of doubt, and no doubt also of its having stimulated those already engaged in the work of reform to fresh efforts, and roused many others to some comprehension of their duty to their fellow creatures.

It is seldom possible to look through the history of men whose lives or deeds have been recorded without lighting on some good point or trait in their characters; but study the lives and histories of the Kelly gang as readers will, it is doubtful whether any such trait will be here found. They were criminals of the deepest dye, and even as children were always a trouble to their neighbours and the police. From the age of between thirteen and fourteen years Ned Kelly proved a thorn in the side of the police stationed near him—by whom, too, he was regarded as an incorrigible thief. He was associated with Power the bushranger in more than one of this latter individuals depredatory excursions, and became an apt pupil. Indeed, when a glance is given at the record of the family, and the kindred spirits with whom they became matrimonially connected, the wonder is that the Kelly gang did not become more notorious even than they did. The father, John Kelly, better known among his confederates as "Red Kelly", as before stated, was a convict from Ireland, and here became notorious as a cattle stealer. His last sentence was completed only a short time before his death. His wife, one of the daughters of John Quin, was in every way worthy of him, and the lawlessness of the children was what might have been expected from the progeny of such a degraded couple. Mrs. Kelly's sisters found as congenial spirits for life companions as she did. Two of them married into the Lloyd family, another became Mrs. Pat Quin. Beside the outlaws, the Kellys had five children. James was well known to the police; Mrs. Skillian and Kate Kelly were the open and avowed enemies of all members of the force, and assisted the gang to keep their enemies at bay; and the family circle was completed by Mrs. Gunn and Grace Kelly. Dan Kelly was a thorough scamp, and while credited with being the most bloodthirsty of the gang, combined in himself all the lowest and most cunning traits in human nature. From such an one as this last few would have expected any but the death of a craven, yet, as the reader knows, he met it with a courage his vainglorious brother Ned did not by any means display. So far as can be ascertained, the manner of his death was the only thing in the whole history that redounded in any way to Dan Kelly's credit.

With such antecedents as they could boast, the marvel would have been if any of the Kelly family even professed respectability in any shape or form. As birds of feather flock together, so Steve

Hart naturally gravitated towards the Kellys and their manner of life. He somewhat resembled Dan Kelly in disposition, and was as much addicted to laying hands on other people's property as the rest of the gang. Joe Byrne had not the excuse of hereditary criminality. He was of respectable family and superior bringing up. He was apparently the educated member of the gang, but, to again quote the Commission report:—"When sixteen years of age he was in trouble, and seems to have developed vicious and cruel propensities." In the bushranging career he chose there was ample scope for any such propensities, and his generally greater knowledge must have been of much service to the gang.

Aaron Sherritt was no whit superior in morals to those he afterwards sought to betray. Superintendent Hare describes him as a "most outrageous scoundrel, and wholly given up to a disreputable life." It must have been a merciful dispensation of Providence that he did not join with the Kelly gang in all their enterprises. Had he done so they must have been even more successful in defying the law and working woe than they were. He resembled Ned Kelly in so many ways that had the two elected to go bushranging together the gang's record would have been still more fearful than it was. Fortunately for the colony at large they did not do so, and from being the staunch friend and ally of the gang, Aaron Sherritt changed front and became one with their pursuers, though it is impossible to discover the exact reason for this change. That the large reward offered had something to do with it was evident; at the same time there might have been that falling out among thieves that would account for its suddenness.

Superintendent Hare put it down to his own personal influence; but men of Sherritt's stamp do not often yield to personality alone. More especially when there was such an incentive to faith-keeping as Aaron's strong and undoubted friendship for Joe Byrne. The change came after he had refused to join them in a raid on a bank in New South Wales. Whether the refusal provoked a quarrel which set Aaron Sherritt at odds with those he had hitherto so staunchly assisted, is not possible to say; but certain it is that from that time he worked so earnestly with the police that he overcame the natural distrust and prejudice the force had against him.

The assault upon Constable Fitzpatrick, the Board of Enquiry held, had precipitated the outbreak, by which they recognised that things were ripe for such a climax, and it is interesting to note how easy and rapid the downward progress in crime becomes. When the Kellys took to the bush after the attack upon Fitzpatrick, they may have thought that the affair would blow over, and relied for their eventual freedom on the terrorism exercised by the Quins, the Lloyds, and the other lawless and desperate characters who resorted to their mother's house. When, however, that mother—with Skillian and Williamson—were imprisoned for lengthy terms, they realised that punishment was being meted out in earnest. When they did this, the advisability of keeping to the wilds, from which they emerged such hardened and resolute offenders, made itself apparent. They were lost to the public sight from that time forth, until they made an unwelcome reappearance at the fatal affair in the Wombat Ranges.

In partial justification of this, Ned Kelly said it was all through Fitzpatrick, and he professed to feel the treatment meted out to his mother very much; but it was evident all through that Constable Fitzpatrick was used only as a scapegoat. The Wombat murders were said to be unpremeditated, and even the Commission decided that there seemed no reason for believing it to be otherwise. For these murders the gang were outlawed, and thenceforward they attempted to mould their lives on those of highwaymen of old. Mr. Hare, after commenting on their general freehandedness, observes:—"And apart from this money consideration, there was a further one which appealed quite as effectively to their humble admirers. The gang never behaved badly to or assaulted a woman, but always treated them with consideration and respect. In like manner they seldom, if ever, made a victim of a poor man; and thus they created a certain halo of romance and rough chivalry around themselves, which to them was worth a great deal— much as did probably the British highwayman of the last century."

It was by such consideration and their own generally good policy that the gang owed its long and, to the colony, costly term of freedom. Their "humble admirers" repaid them by information regarding to the movements of the police, by provisions and assistance in various ways. That the gang had more than one narrow escape isevident, and what was described as fatality often proved to be nothing less than blundering, and, when not brought about by want of nerve, indolence or incompetence could be generally looked upon as the cause of the trouble of the hour. The "Sebastopol Charge" subjected all connected in it to ridicule, and made the police the laughing-stock of all the colonies; and the failure of the Warby Ranges expedition roused general indignation. The gang would not have been able to evade their pursuers had anything like ordinary promptitude been displayed in regard to them. As it was not, the outlaws must have been very much encouraged by their success. They were, according to all accounts, worn and wet and weary. They narrowly escaped drowning, and in coming back were delayed long enough for the pursuing party to have at least caught up to them. This was attempted a day after, but of course without result, and the gang went on their way, it may be assumed, rejoicing. The next event— the Euroa Bank robbery—revealed something of the systematic capacity of the gang; and in the raid on the bank at Jerilderie their business-like method and coolness had as much to do with the paralysing of all thought of resistance as their revolvers.

The career of the Kelly gang shows one long and costly record of official incapacity; and the way in which censure and punishment was meted out all round when the time came for it, must have convinced the somewhat sceptical public that the desire to deal out even-handed justice was both earnest and strong. The "indolence and incompetence" of Inspector Brook Smith, the personal feuds and petty jealousies of Messrs. Nicholson and Hare, and, later on, the unpleasantness among the officers in regard to the black trackers, and the want of impartiality, temper, tact and judgment evinced by the Chief Commissioner (Captain Standish) in dealing with his subordinates, were all fully taken into account. Superintendent Sadlier was also censured for errors of judgment, and harsh and unmerited treatment of subordinates; and Sergeant Steele came in for very great censure for neglecting to take action when the gang were seen at Wangaratta. Detective Ward was held to have been guilty of misleading superior officers on several occasions during the pursuit; and the constables who were in Sherritt's hut on the night of the murder were condemned in the strongest language that official etiquette would permit. Senior Constables Kelly and Johnson, who had been most harshly treated by Superintendent Sadlier, were recommended for promotion, as well as Constable Bracken, whose promptitude and coolness at Glenrowan, were regarded as having in a great measure led to the destruction of the gang on that occasion. Mr. Curnow, who prevented the wrecking of the special train, was singled out for special praise, and the bravery of Mr. Rawlings was warmly recognised. Mr. Wallace, a State school teacher at Hurdle Creek, who had been active as a Kelly sympathiser, and was credited with being the writer of an anonymous letter written to the Chief Commissioner of Police, and reflecting strongly on Mr. Nicholson's character and conduct, was unsparingly criticised, and his immediate dismissal from the Education Department recommended.

This evident official incompetence, in conjunction with the hardiness and consequent daring of the Kelly gang, makes their long immunity from arrest less a matter of surprise. They were, according to accounts, hardy in the extreme. Aaron Sherritt—who was, in Mr. Hare's opinion, exceptionally so—said that Ned Kelly was ten times as hardy as himself. The most severe weather seems to have had but little effect on them. In the attempt to cross the Murray they had much to endure, and for some time previous to the outbreak at Glenrowan it was known that they were suffering great hardships, and that they were obliged to get a tent to cover them at night; but they were apparently as hardened physically as they were mentally. Their strength, too, must have been something phenomenal, or they could never have supported or moved about in the armor in which they encased themselves. Of this the *Argus* says:—"An examination of the armor worn by Edward Kelly and his three comrades showed it to be of a most substantial character. It was made of iron a quarter of an inch thick, and consisted of a long breast-plate, shoulder-plates, back-guard, and helmet. The helmet resembled a nail-can without a crown, and was made with a long slit at the elevation of the eyes to enable the wearer to look through. All these articles are believed to have been made by two men—one living near Greta, the other near Oxley. The iron was procured by the larceny of ploughshares. Petty robberies of this kind having been frequent in the Kelly district, the police had begun to suspect the gang were preparing for renewed action. Ned Kelly's armor alone weighed 97 lbs., and those who saw it ceased to wonder at the singular immunity from injury the desperado enjoyed in his fight with the police."

It was the opinion of Mr. Hare that had the outlaws not worn armor none of those who first attacked the hotel could have escaped being shot. The outlaws could not take proper aim when encumbered by their armor, as they were obliged to hold the rifle at arm's length. To the front breast-plate of Ned Kelly's armor a flap was attached, and the whole was so clumsy in appearance, and so weighty, that it is evident he had no alternative but to act as he did at Glenrowan. He could not disencumber himself of his armor without assistance from others, so he made his sensational return to the hotel. His capture forms one of the most exciting of the sensational incidents with which the history abounds. That the flight that ensued was a desperate one is evidenced by the bullet marks that were found on his armor. When it was taken off and examined five were found on the helmet, three on the breast-plate, nine on the back-plate, and one on the shoulder-plate. Our illustrations of these are from the *Australian Sketcher,* permission to copy having been readily and most courteously accorded, and the more they are studied the more incredible does it seem that human beings were able to move and breathe under such burdens. No 1 in the illustration, is a front view of the helmet; No. 2, the head piece, viewed from the side; No. 3, represents the breast-plate; No. 4, the plate used for the protection of the back; No. 5, the back lappet; and No. 6, the front view of the whole. This armor is still carefully preserved in Melbourne.

The suit worn by Dan Kelly is kept at the Treasury Buildings, as well as some portions of, presumably, that worn by Joe Byrne. Steve Hart's armor is one of the attractions of the Armory Court at the Aquarium, and the suit in which Ned Kelly defied the police for so long on the last memorable day of his bushranging existence is in the possession of Sir William Clarke, of Sunbury, and "Clivedon", East Melbourne. The more this armor is looked at, felt, and weighed, the more one wonders, how any human beings could live, move, or breathe under such a weight of cold iron. The illustrations are as exact as it is possible to be, but the armor has to be seen ere its weight and dimensions can be realised. The Victorian Government should certainly endeavor to secure the whole four suits, as they form relics most unique of the most unique phase in the history of Victoria.

It is not so wonderful that Ned Kelly when thus protected should have escaped with comparatively few wounds from the number of shots that were fired by his assailants. "Very brave", "very plucky," was the stand made against the police regarded by the lower orders; but had Ned Kelly been minus his armor he most probably would not have been there. Early in the day he had, it was asserted, shot at a defenceless old man, Martin Cherry, and wounded him mortally for refusing to draw and hold aside a window-blind so that Ned Kelly might fire at the police. Martin Cherry was by far the most heroic of the two, for when he refused to do as he was ordered he must have known that he did so at the risk of his life.

The contest between Ned Kelly and nine policemen lasted for half an hour, and the number of shots fired in that time must have been far and away beyond the number of wounds afterwards found to have been inflicted. The outlaw was wounded several times in the right leg, once in the left foot, and once on the right hand. There were also two wounds on the right arm and two near the groin.

The gang had so much the advantage of the police in the first of the attack at Glenrowan that more lives would undoubtedly have been sacrificed had they been unencumbered, and so able to aim with their usual fatal sureness. The hotel and the men stationed on the verandah were in deep shadow; the police were in the light given by the waning moon, but evidently plainly discernible to those who were bent on destroying some of their enemies as well as defending themselves.

Dean Gibney, it will be remembered, was the priest who, with the devotion which has been the marked characteristic of men of his class, displayed it in his determination to rescue Martin Cherry from a dreadful death. That this rescue did not save the unfortunate man from death was due to the nature of his wounds; but he was at all events spared the horrors of a death by fire, which, of all others, surely is the most fearful. The evidence of Father Gibney, given before the Commission, reflected anything but favourably on the judgment and generalship displayed in the destruction of the Kelly gang at Glenrowan, and the Commission were very much in accord with many of the unfavourable opinions hazarded by spectators of this final scene.

Of this priest the late Mr. Julian Thomas, who under his well known *nom the plume* of "The Vagabond" had published an account of journeyings in Western Australia shortly before his death on the 4th September of this year, wrote when writing of Perth:—"Occasionally one sees the Church represented on St. George's Terrace. Bishop Riley, of the Church of England, sometimes takes the air here. So, too, does Bishop Gibney, of the Catholic Church. I have very great pleasure in meeting Dr. Gibney. He is a man as well as a Bishop. Dr. Gibney was the young priest who was first to enter the inn at Glenrowan when the Kelly outlaws had possession of it. I had long heard of this dramatic incident, and wondered what had become of the young priest. It is a pleasing surprise to find him Bishop of Perth. When I mention the Glenrowan episode to him there is at first a sad look in his eyes, which changes to a humorous one as he says, 'I suppose you think it is only one of my countrymen who would join the bushrangers.' I recognise in Bishop Gibney one who has the greatest sympathy with 'the griefs and joys that weave the weft of Time.' "

It seems almost incredible that nearly fifty police could have been kept at bay by three men who were armed with very defective weapons, and sheltered only in what was practically little more than a hut. The manifest difficulty in lighting on some means of bringing matters to a climax would not have impressed those present with anything but a disbelief in the capacity and resource of those sworn to defend and protect the people. The suggestion of a wooden bullet-proof shield to be attached to a dray or wagon, so that the attacking party might approach the house in safety and effect its ruin, seems not to have been entertained, so that the night dragged its weary length along, until the destruction of the gang was at length accomplished.

It is hardly likely that another Ned Kelly will arise. There are, no doubt, many endowed with much the same hardihood and inclinations, as well as the same kind of so-called courage, but conditions now are hardly so favourable for their performance as in the days of the Kelly gang. The lawless of the community were daunted by the fearful end three of the gang came to, and the hanging of one to whom most of their crimes were traceable.

There was now nothing for the Victorian Government to do in this matter but insist on a complete reorganisation of the police force, and this probably more than anything else had the effect of keeping in check those wishing to emulate the doings of the Kelly gang. The revelation of the ignorance and crime that flourished near the much boasted civilisation has not been without its effect, and the romance and glamour that surrounded the members of the gang has been dispelled by the knowledge of their privations and the fearfully hard life they had to suffer owing to the price set upon their heads.

In this compilation much assistance has been derived from the columns of the papers of the day; also from the very clear account of the proceedings of the gang given by Mr. Otto Berliner. In the destruction of the Kelly gang there was also the destruction of much that had made bushranging attractive to the young and lawlessly aspiring imagination, as well as to the older and more criminally inclined. Many threats were indulged in as the bodies of Hart and Dan Kelly were handed over to their friends for interment; and one relative of the Kellys, it was averred, held up his hand over the bodies of the two and vowed to Kate Kelly that he would avenge the slaughter of the gang—for slaughter the Kelly friends and sympathisers elected to regard it. The scene at Greta when the dead bodies arrived, and were taken to Mrs. Skillian's hut, was something unparalleled. The excitement throughout the district was most intense, and Mrs. Skillian's hut was rushed. This was too much for the owner's equanimity, and like a true Kelly she seized a gun and soon cleared the shanty. There was a great wake over the remains. A large quantity of liquor had been procured at Glenrowan, and the Kelly family and sympathisers, who were armed, and all more or less intoxicated, threatened to attack the police. They did not do so, but it was deemed advisable not to hold the usual magisterial enquiries. In the state most of those in the district were then in it could not have been done without danger of bloodshed. At first it was thought that an investigation had better take place, but there was manifest unwillingness to undertake the enquiry on the part of those who would have to go through with it. After discussion and some delay it was resolved that a magistrate, with four troopers and two or three Wangaratta police should proceed to Mrs. Skillian's hut. But the probable consequences at last decided the authorities to omit the enquiries, which were of a purely formal and, under the circumstances, unnecessary proceeding. This undoubtedly was the wisest course, and a magistrate's order for interment was accordingly despatched to Greta; the police were recalled, and the danger was over. The sympathisers had declared their intention to inter the bodies at a certain time, whether enquiries had been held or not; and Dick Hart, it was declared, had dared the police to interfere with the funerals, and had said:—"If you want the bodies back, you will have to fight for them." Police, magistrates, and all concerned, however, had had too much of fighting to needlessly provoke this choice company, so the Greta friends of the dead did as they would with the bodies.

It was for a time thought that the talk of blowing up the police camp and bank at Benalla, after the special train and its occupants were destroyed, was only idle boast, but the discovery of a can of blasting powder at McDonnell's Hotel, and of the fuses in the outlaws' swags, was proof of how deadly in earnest they were.

It is all past now, however; the dangers and the Kellys are alike removed, and there can be no apprehension of any such gang of desperadoes again disturbing the public peace of Victoria. In the whole of their history there is nothing to move to admiration or in any way lighten the effect of it. If there was one amusing incident in the whole pitiable proceedings it was that described in *The Sketcher* when dealing with the surrender and escape of those imprisoned in Jones's hotel. Referring thereto, this journal said:—"The scene presented when all were lying on the ground, demonstrating their respectability of character, was unique and in some degree amusing." It must have been, for they were all lying prone on their stomachs, with head and one hand up, all in as much fear apparently of the police as of the outlaws.

In the compiling of the of the foregoing account of one of the most sensational and exciting episodes in the history of the colony of Victoria much thought and labor has been bestowed to render it historically correct as well as make it interesting. Thorough search has been made through the newspapers of the time, the various books published on the subject, and also the Government Commission Report. From these much assistance has been derived, and by their aid the strange eventful history of the Kelly gang has been made as complete as possible.

THE END.

Printed in Australia
AUHW010651040319
309362AU00002B/4